$1.95

Cat. No. ABC-1

ABC's OF COMPUTERS

by

ALLAN LYTEL

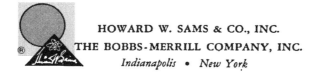

HOWARD W. SAMS & CO., INC.

THE BOBBS-MERRILL COMPANY, INC.

Indianapolis • *New York*

PREFACE

Future historians may herald our civilization as the "second industrial revolution." Just as the first industrial revolution created machines that unharnessed man from the shackles of manual labor, so will electronic computers ultimately free him from the drudgery of ordinary mental labor in computation and record keeping. Already, computers are keeping up-to-the-minute accounts of deposits and withdrawals in banks, computing and making out payroll checks in business offices, and running oil refineries that are fully automated from raw product to tank car.

ABC'S of Computers is a basic introduction to computers. In easy-to-understand language it explains what they are, how they operate, and what they can be expected to do. It is written to serve as a self-teaching text for those who want to gain an overall understanding of modern computers.

The two basic types of computers—digital and analog—are described. Also included are simplified explanations of circuits, numbering systems, arithmetic operations, symbolic logic, logic circuits, counters, memory storage, input and output devices, and programming.

This book is based, in part, on my teaching experiences at Temple University Technical Institute and Community College and at International Business Machines, both in Philadelphia.

Thanks to the cooperation of numerous computer manufacturers who so generously supplied the illustrative material, it was possible to make the contents represent the current state of the art.

In 1956, Mr. Ralph J. Cordiner, president of General Electric, commented that the three important contributions of our age are nuclear energy, automation, and computers. A more fitting reason for writing this book could not be found.

ALLAN LYTEL

February, 1961

TABLE OF CONTENTS

CHAPTER 1

Computers –
Digital and Analog

A few short years ago, the computer was reserved for complicated scientific calculations. Today, however, they are more important to our everyday lives than most of us realize. A computer may already make out your paycheck, record your insurance premium, process your department-store bill, or address the magazine you subscribe to.

Modern digital computers are fast—so fast that their speed is almost beyond the grasp of human understanding. Some can perform *one billion* operations a second, and even faster computers are on the way. Scientific problems which formerly required years to solve, can be computed in days or hours by digital computers. Many such problems have even been reduced to minutes.

Computation is only one aspect of modern computers, however. Other uses are to control machine tools and to translate languages. One computer, in the laboratory stage, will translate from one language to another at the fantastic speed of 1800 words per minute! (An average human translator can do only about 2500 words a day.) Another experimental computer (automatic digit recognizer) can translate spoken words into actual commands and then obey them.

Automation, or the completely automatic production of finished goods from start to finish, is made possible by computers. Heavy-duty milling machines, drill presses, and lathes are being controlled entirely by electronics. These control systems prepare magnetic recording tapes directly from numerical data and control entire machining cycles in the following manner.

A device reads this data to the machine, which is controlled in accordance with the commands. The machine also stores the programs for repetitive operations and runs them as many times as needed. A typical industrial computer can save about half the machining time formerly taken by manual operations.

The computer provides continuous pulses which command the machine tool to move along a specified path at the proper speed, maintaining proper co-ordination at all times, and "tells" the cutting tools when and where to make their cuts. The computer operates at very high speeds, and one computer can provide control tapes for a number of different machine tools.

Computers can also "talk" to each other by means of microwave links and telephone wires. Their answers are helping to cut the cost of big rocket engines in one example. They are saving engineers hundreds of hours of experimentation and testing, and are giving management the daily status of every program.

They also are spotting potential trouble in budgets, in time for something to be done. The engineering laboratories at one location are connected to test stands in other states, and are linked by leased wires or microwaves to electronic computers at headquarters. These computers exchange information at the rate of 75,000 words per minute!

Other computers produce graph reports which show management the budget status of every project, or keep a running inventory of the thousands of parts required in production. Any of this information is available in minutes on demand.

Thus it is easy to understand why computers are being increasingly used as tools for science, engineering, inventory control, manufacturing—or indeed, for almost any business or industrial application.

TYPES OF COMPUTERS

There are two types of computers: The analog computer *measures* a quantity (as does a voltmeter), and the digital computer *counts* numbers (as does an adding machine). In an analog system, quantities are measured rather than counted before being fed to the inputs. The computer acts on the inputs, performing a number of mathematical operations or solving an equation, and plots the output data on a graph.

In contrast, suppose you want to multiply two numbers by using logarithms. You must first look up their logarithms in a table. Then you add the log of the first number to the log of the second, and their sum is the log of the number you would have gotten had you multiplied the original numbers. But a slide rule does the same thing much faster mechanically, since it is really only a table of logarithms (and also an elementary form of computer).

An *analog computer*, like the slide rule, is simpler and more direct than a digital computer, but ordinarily is not a high-precision device. It functions at its best when a precision of three or four digits is sufficient, program flexibility is not important, and there is only one independent variable. Data available in analog form, such as a varying voltage representing temperature or speed, can be fed directly to an analog computer. However,

8

its disadvantages—lack of precision and limited flexibility—are usually not sufficient to overcome this advantage. To run a different problem, an analog computer usually must be reconnected by means of interconnecting patch cords.

A *digital computer,* like an adding machine, counts rather than measures. It is really an ultrahigh-speed electronic calculating machine. One way of looking at the difference between the two is to say the digital computer works with integers and the analog computer does not. In construction, both consist of many basic electronic circuits put together like building blocks.

ANALOG COMPUTERS

Analog computers use basic relationships between two varying voltages to provide an analogous representation, as seen from Fig. 1-1. Consider this circuit an FM detector in which the currents flow through R1 and R2 in opposite directions. Voltmeter M1 reads the drop across R1, and M2 the drop across R2. If these resistances are equal and the currents are also equal, the two

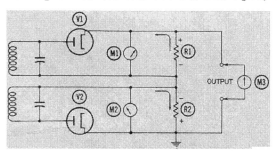

Fig. 1-1. Analog addition.

voltages will be equal but of opposite polarity. The total voltage will read zero on M3 because the outputs are connected series-opposing and therefore cancel each other.

However, if the voltage read on M1 (designated E_1) exceeds the voltage read on M2 (E_2), the resulting voltage will be positive; if E_2 exceeds E_1, this voltage will be negative. Thus, this circuit is an *algebraic adder,* the output of which is a voltage comprising the sum of the two inputs and taking into consideration their respective signs. This circuit can be written algebraically as $E_3 = E_1 - E_2$.

The circuit shown has no amplifier, although amplifiers are used in many analog-computer circuits. These amplifiers are high-gain stages which can perform many operations. Fig. 1-2 shows one example. By the use of simple networks a single stage (actu-

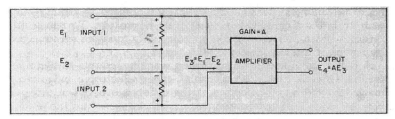

Fig. 1-2. Analog multiplication.

ally, two tubes) can perform such operations as addition or multiplication. In Fig. 1-2 the amplifier input is the E_3 of Fig. 1-1. The output (E_4) is equal to the input (E_3) times the gain of the stage. Suppose the gain is 12 and the input is +6 volts. The output will then be 12 × 6, or 72 volts. Subtraction (negative addition) and division (multiplication with less than unity gain) can all be accomplished in the same direct fashion.

An analog computer is shown in Fig. 1-3. On the left, below the table, are the power supplies. Amplifiers are in the panels to the

Fig. 1-3. An analog computer.

right, while controls for setting in the problem are shown on the table top and the sloping panel. The patch cords (upper right) interconnect the appropriate computer sections for a specific problem.

Analog computers do many jobs. An installation of an Air Force Air Traffic Control system uses an analog computer to track aircraft and schedule their landings, at a rate of two a minute, so they do not interfere with each other. The computer calculates the proper flight path for each aircraft, while the operators insert values indicating wind direction and velocity, the proper runway to be used, and the heading of the aircraft. After this is done, the computer compares the actual path of the aircraft with the theoretical path it has plotted, and then relays any corrections.

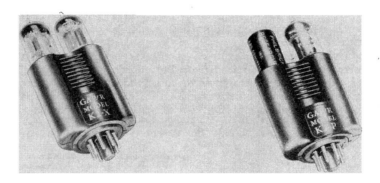

Fig. 1-4. Two plug-in amplifiers.

Are analog computers complex? Actually they are not—in addition to power supplies, their main components are amplifiers (Fig. 1-4) and passive networks of resistors, capacitors, and inductors (Fig. 1-5). By connecting the proper amplifiers and passive networks, it is possible to represent any problem.

Since an analog computer measures but does not count, quantities may be represented in several ways. A mechanical representation is shown in Fig. 1-6A. The shaft turns the pinion, moving the rack a certain distance corresponding to the quantity: A large quantity means a large movement; a small number, a correspondingly smaller movement. Electrically a variable resistance, as in Fig. 1-6B, gives the same result. As the shaft turns to represent a number, a voltage is provided at the output. The regulated voltage input provides a reference source for the entire resistance.

Figs. 1-1 and 1-2 have shown how addition or subtraction can be done in a single stage of the computer. But a complex opera-

Fig. 1-5. Four passive plug-in networks.

tion such as integration or differentiation can also be accomplished in just one stage.

The rate of change of a voltage, E, with respect to time is called its derivative (one is *derived* from the other). Examples of the use of a derivative, in problems to be solved on an analog computer, are velocity (the rate of change of *distance* with respect to time) and acceleration (the rate of change of *velocity*, again with respect to time). Thus a derivative represents the rate of

(A) Mechanical.   (B) Electrical.

Fig. 1-6. Two ways of representing a quantity.

change with respect to some variable, usually time. Finding the derivative is called differentiation.

Integration—the opposite of differentiation—is the method by which the computer produces a sum at any varying rate. The capacitor is the basic summing device. The electrical charge is fed to (or removed from) it at a controlled rate. The voltage across the capacitor rises as its charge increases and, at any instant, is the integral of the charging rate. In other words, the charging rate is deliberately controlled in order to represent the number or quantity to be integrated.

Integration, as shown in Fig. 1-7A, uses capacitor C to store the charge received. The voltage across C is, at any instant, the

12

integral of the charging rate. This circuit computes the time integral of the input. An amplifier is added (Fig. 1-7B) to prevent removal of the charge on C during integration.

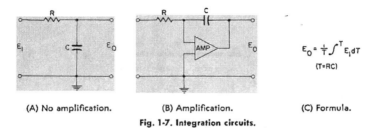

(A) No amplification. (B) Amplification. (C) Formula.

$$E_0 = \frac{1}{T} \int^T E_i \, dT$$
(T=RC)

Fig. 1-7. Integration circuits.

The inverse of integration is, of course, differentiation, or the determination of the rate at which one quantity changes with respect to another quantity, usually time. The circuit in Fig. 1-8A is a simple type of differentiator. In Fig. 1-8B an amplifier which has resistive feedback is used.

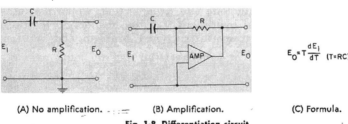

(A) No amplification. (B) Amplification. (C) Formula.

$$E_0 = T \frac{dE_i}{dT} \quad (T=RC)$$

Fig. 1-8. Differentiation circuit.

DIGITAL COMPUTERS

Digital computers are of many sizes and shapes, just as they perform many different functions. A cash register and an abacus are both digital computers. In a digital computer, quantities are *counted*, rather than measured as in an analog computer. Because numbers are used, any degree of precision can be obtained simply by carrying more digits. Since digits are used, the computer components (transistors, vacuum tubes, etc.) respond to *on* or *off* states—like a switch which is either open or closed—and thus can represent a *0* or a *1*.

Fig. 1-9 shows a digital computer used for inventory control. Its calculating circuits are rather simple, but it has a very large memory in order to store the huge quantities of data required for this purpose. A typical installation for a computer that does payroll records and billing is shown in Fig. 1-10.

13

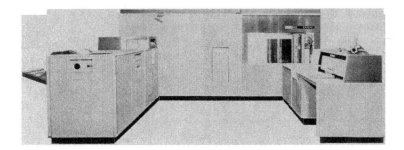

Fig. 1-9. The IBM 305 RAMAC digital computer.

In many respects a digital computer is a kind of automatic calculating device which not only can follow instructions, but can remember a whole series of them as well. Most digital computers can be represented by the block diagram in Fig. 1-11. There are, of course, variations of this fundamental computer. The basic units are: (1) the arithmetic and logic section, which performs the actual arithmetical operations, (2) the memory, or storage, which retains the program (instructions), problem, and solution,

Fig. 1-10. The NCR Model 304 digital computer.

(3) the control unit, which directs the computer's operation, (4) the input devices, for translating into usable form all input information, and (5) the output device, which translates the computer's output into a form understandable by the operator.

14

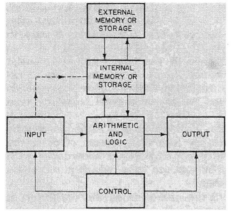

Fig. 1-11. Block diagram of a digital computer.

The *arithmetic unit,* or accumulator, gathers information, and under the computer's control, acts on this data which it either has stored itself or which it recalls from the memory unit. For example, a number from the memory can be placed in the accumulator. Upon receipt of an order such as AND (explained later in the chapter), a number will be added to the one already in the accumulator, which then contains the sum. Depending on the problem, this sum can be transferred to the memory, or it can be retained by the accumulator for further operations. In the case of a negative number, the accumulator will recognize the negative sign. For a "subtract" operation, the accumulator finds the difference and attaches the proper sign. To "multiply," a series of additions is made in the accumulator, and to "divide," a series of subtractions. The series, or sequence, of operations is a *program;* and the individual steps are *instructions.*

The *memory,* or *storage,* unit has a large number of individual locations, or addresses, each capable of storing information until needed. Each location can be described and located, so that either its information, or else the new location where the information is stored, can be obtained. A specific group of addresses is called a *register.* Reading out a piece of information from the memory does not destroy the data—the same information can be referred to indefinitely. In a digital computer, all the information needed for a solution to a problem can be stored in the memory, including all the steps or the program required for the solution. Once the proper information has been placed in the memory, the computer is independent of all outside devices until a solution is reached. At this time the final results are stored until needed, and then are presented through the output device.

15

The basic internal memory is a group of magnetic cores. Magnetic tapes, shown at the left in Fig. 1-10, are an important type of secondary storage. Data are read from a tape, or to a tape, to supplement the core memory.

Magnetic drums, another type of secondary storage, consist of a rotating metal drum around which are several tracks of recording material similar to magnetic tape. One or more heads for each track record or read pulse information from the tape as the drum rotates.

Other memories include the Williams tube, a cathode-ray tube on which data are stored on the face in the form of dots; the capacitor store, the charge of which changes in accordance with the digital data; a transistor or vacuum tube, which is either on for a 1 or off for a 0; plus others.

The *control section* directs the operation of the computer in order to fulfill the conditions set forth by the program. The control unit observes the instructions and plans their proper execution by following the principles of operation for a given machine. For example, this selection may translate a "multiply" order into a series of additions (which it actually is to the computer).

Input and *output* devices are similar in operation, but perform opposite functions. An input unit reads information from punched cards, magnetic tapes, or keyboards. It also codes this data so that the computer can handle and use the information. The opposite function is performed by the output unit; it converts the computer results into a form usable by the operator, such as typed sheets, or punched cards for the control of production machines.

Two operations of this typical computer will give some insight into its function. Suppose the program command says "divide 1100 by 250." Being unable to divide, the arithmetic section subtracts 250 from 1100, then subtracts 250 from the remainder, and so on, until the remainder is less than the divisor, as follows:

$$
\begin{array}{ll}
1100 & \\
\underline{250} & \\
850 & \text{once} \\
\underline{250} & \\
600 & \text{twice} \\
\underline{250} & \\
350 & \text{three times} \\
\underline{250} & \\
100 & \text{four times}
\end{array}
$$

After four subtractions, the remainder is 100. Hence the computer counts the number of subtractions (four), and provides the answer at the output—1100 divided by 250 is 4, with a remainder of 100.

Multiplication is a series of additions; hence, to multiply 2500 by 4, the computer proceeds as follows:

```
  2500  once
  2500
  ————
  5000  twice
  2500
  ————
  7500  three times
  2500
  ——————
 10,000  four times
```

Thus, 2500 is added four times to give the proper answer, 10,000.

Decimal-system numbers have been used in the examples here; however, most modern computers employ binary numbers.

. **Binary Numbers**

Numbering systems go back almost to the beginning of civilized man. Because we have 10 fingers, our numbering system is based on 10. But other numbering concepts are possible; and some are more useful for electronic systems, where a relay is either open or closed, an indicator lamp is on or off, a vacuum tube either conducts or does not, or a transistor has a pulse output or no output. Based on these bistable, or two-state, devices the binary (2-number) system has been made the basis for the modern digital computer, which is really a high-speed electronic calculator. The binary (powers of 2) system uses only two digits, 0 and 1.

Both computations and instructions for computer operations are in the form of binary numbers. Unlike mechanical devices such as counters, which can be based on the decimal system, electronic devices for modern digital computers usually have only two states—on and off. Early computers used relays; now transistors or vacuum tubes are used as switches in computers.

For mechanization, the decimal system of numbering (to the base 10) requires ten different and recognizable states, one for each digit. In general, any numbering system requires m states, where m is the numbering base. Since a vacuum tube or transistor normally has only two stable states that are dependable, 10 tubes (or transistors) would be needed to represent the decimal digits of 0 through 9.

To overcome these difficulties, the binary numbering system was adapted for use in industrial control systems and digital computers. It is based on successive powers of 2, and only two digits

17

Table 1-1. Binary representation of numbers.

Decimal	Binary		
	2^2	2^1	2^0
0	0	0	0
1	0	0	1
2	0	1	0
3	0	1	1
4	1	0	0

—1 and 0—are used. Table 1-1 gives the binary representation for the decimal numbers 0, 1, 2, 3, and 4. Starting at the right of the table, the first column represents 2^0, or decimal 1. The next column is 2^1, or decimal 2; and the third is 2^2, or 4. Thus, decimal 3 for example is binary 011, which means no 4's, one 2, and one 1. Likewise, binary 101 is decimal 5—or one 4, no 2's, and one 1.

Symbolic Logic

The rules of binary arithmetic provide a complete system of numbers which can be used for counting. There are several advantages to this two-value system, compared with other numbering bases. Rules are quite direct and simple; for example, there are no tables for multiplication. For use in computers, binary numbers also have the advantage of requiring only two states of the indicators, which are vacuum tubes or transistors. The ON and OFF states can be used to represent the 1 and 0 of the binary system, respectively.

The manipulation of numbers can be treated through use of logical connectives which mean OR or AND. In logic, OR has two meanings. If A is one event and B is another, then "A OR B" can mean either one event, A; or if not A, then B. But this is not the only meaning of the word OR. If event A occurs and, at the same time, event B also occurs, this satisfies the condition of A OR B. Thus the two meanings are: (1) either A or B, but not both; (2) either A or B, or both. In other words, OR actually means and/or (either A or B, or both A and B). Where A is one binary number and B is a second number, A plus B (A + B), which is addition, can be considered as A OR B.

In the same manner, A times B (A · B), which is multiplication, can be considered as A AND B. Thus, logical AND is binary multiplication; and logical OR is binary addition. Together with the concept of negation (not-A, not-B), the OR-AND conditions may be used for computer logic, as you will learn in later chapters.

CHAPTER 2

Tube and Relay
Switching Devices

In this chapter we will look at some of the active circuit elements in computers. All digital computers, whether large or small, are only collections of switching circuits arranged in a functional and logical manner. Because of the "on-off" characteristics of most switching devices, the binary (two-valued) numbering system is used.

Switching circuits in digital-computer systems represent the two-valued system by "on-off," or "open-closed." Vacuum tubes or transistors operate as simple switches which either permit current flow or do not permit current flow. These switching devices have but two states and hence cannot easily be made to represent the 10-state decimal system. Other switching devices are also used, including relays, semiconductor diodes, and magnetics.

In digital-computer computation, many individual operations of addition or subtraction are required. These fundamental operations occur in the arithmetic unit.

COMPUTER SWITCHING

The arithmetic unit is made up of a large number of individual two-state devices called stages. One of these is the gate.

The gate is the descriptive name for a type of circuit switch which can be open or closed. It has a number of possible inputs, and an output signal is provided only if certain conditions are met by the input signal. There are two types of gates: The AND gate provides an output only when *all* input signals are present. The OR gate, or buffer, provides an output if *any* input signals are present.

The bistable circuit, or flip-flop, is another fundamental building block of the computer. Flip-flops can be made from vacuum tubes, transistors, or other active devices. Each flip-flop circuit has two stable states: the *set* state, or 1; and the *reset* state, or 0. In effect, the set and reset states can be considered similar to the open and closed states of an ordinary switch or relay.

Because of its stable nature in both states, a flip-flop can be used for binary storage. It will hold and remember a bit (binary digit), the set output being 1 and the reset output, 0.

19

Flip-flops can be used for several purposes. One is to store binary information, which includes other than just binary numbers. For example, the flip-flop can store information about the sign of a number (whether it is plus or minus). Since it has two outputs, set and reset, and since there are only two signs, plus and minus, it is easy to see why a flip-flop can indicate the sign of a number.

The shift register is one of the simplest and most frequently-used digital devices. Its applications include temporary storage of digital data, conversion of data from serial to parallel or from parallel to serial, and generation of pulse patterns.

A shift register consists of a number of flip-flops connected together so that each flip-flop transfers its information to the next flip-flop when the advance input is pulsed.

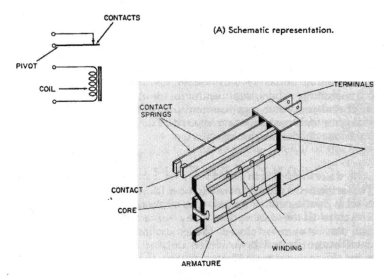

(A) Schematic representation.

(B) Pictorial representation.

Fig. 2-1. A simple relay.

RELAYS

Electromagnetic relays were used as the switching devices in early computers, but their slow speed limited the information rate and hence the computer speed. However, their action will be discussed here to explain the functions of other devices.

A basic electromagnetic relay, shown in Fig. 2-1, consists of a coil wound on an iron core. DC passes through the coil and creates

20

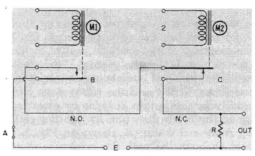

Fig. 2-2. A series relay circuit.

a magnetic field which attracts the iron armature from its support by the spring. Pivoting at the point as indicated, the armature moves and closes the contacts connected to the load. Fig. 2-1A shows the contacts normally closed (N.C.) rather than normally open (N.O.). When the coil is energized, the contacts open. The mechanical structure of a basic relay may be seen from Fig. 2-1B.

Thousands of different relay types, both general and special purpose, are available for different switching applications. Relays are used in a circuit such as that in Fig. 2-2, which demonstrates two logical functions. A, B, and C are in series. Only if all three are closed is there a drop across R. Consider A as closed. As drawn, the circuit (A, B, C) is then open since B is open. If B is closed by energizing relay M1, the circuit will be closed. If after the circuit is closed, relay M2 is energized, contacts C open and this opens the circuit.

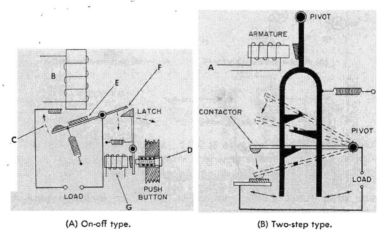

(A) On-off type.   (B) Two-step type.

Fig. 2-3. Two relay latching arrangements.

21

Fig. 2-3A shows a relay latching arrangement. When coil B is energized, armature E is attracted toward it. This action closes contacts C and completes the circuit through the load. Because of the pivoting action, F moves down and is locked in place by the latch (which is held by the spring). Now the contacts will remain closed when the coil is de-energized; a short current flow triggers this locking action and the relay stays closed. It can be opened manually by the button at D, or by electrically attracting the latch bar in the other direction by another coil G.

A latching relay can count, as shown in Fig. 2-3B. Each time current passes through the coil, the armature moves to the left and then is restored by the spring action. For each current pulse at A, the contact bar moves down one notch. As shown here, two on-off sequences are required until the contacts complete the circuit through the load. This is a relay counter using the latch principle. Larger counts are quite possible; but as the number increases, the device becomes more and more complex.

VACUUM AND GAS TUBES

Both vacuum and gas-filled tubes can act as switching circuits. In later chapters these circuits will be more greatly detailed to

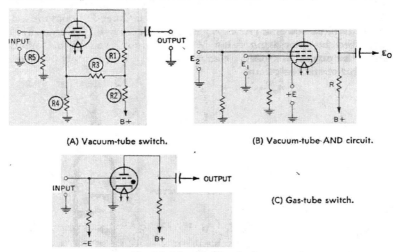

(A) Vacuum-tube switch.　　　(B) Vacuum-tube AND circuit.

(C) Gas-tube switch.

Fig. 2-4. Tube-switching circuits.

show their functions in computers. They are included here to illustrate their use as active circuit elements.

Fig. 2-4 shows three circuits using tubes. In Fig. 2-4A, the tube acts as a switch. Because of voltage divider R2, R3, and R4, the cathode voltage is positive and the tube is normally cut off. Only a positive pulse on the control grid large enough to overcome the bias will allow the tube to conduct and produce an output across R1. Fig. 2-4B shows how a tube can be used as amplifier in an AND configuration. Because of cathode bias E, this tube does not conduct, and a positive signal E_1 on one grid is not enough to cause conduction. But if the other grid also receives a positive voltage (E_2), the tube will conduct and produce an output drop across R. Thus, there will be an output if E_1 and E_2 are both present to overcome cathode bias E.

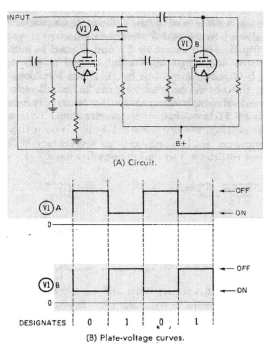

(A) Circuit.

(B) Plate-voltage curves.

Fig. 2-5. The flip-flop circuit.

The triode thyatron in Fig. 2-4C is another type of tube switch. Grid bias keeps the tube from drawing current until a positive input allows the plate voltage to create a current flow. In a thyatron, however, the grid cannot regain control until the plate voltage goes negative.

The flip-flop—a tube switch with two output states—is illustrated in Fig. 2-5. It is a basic computer circuit; the one in Fig. 2-5A is a bistable circuit which works in the following manner.

23

With no input, one tube conducts more heavily and, because of feedback, goes into saturation. Heavy current flow through the cathode resistor is enough to keep the other tube cut off. A positive pulse applied to the grids of both tubes will switch their state. This circuit has two stable states—V1A conducting and V1B off, and V1A off and V1B conducting. Each tube will remain in its latest state until changed by an input.

In order to count, the on-off states require some type of designation. As shown at the bottom of Fig. 2-5B, V1A off and V1B on represents a 0, while V1A on and V1B off is a 1. Thus it takes two pulses for the circuit to reach its original state. In other words, starting with either a 1 or a 0, two pulses are required to return the circuit to its initial condition.

A single flip-flop will count by 2's and is used in series to make counters. Since one stage counts by 2, two stages count by 4, three count by 8, and four count by 16. After 16 pulses to the first stage input, the entire counter returns to its all-zero state. For digital computers which operate on the binary system (as most do), a count by 16 is useful.

CHAPTER 3

Solid-State
Circuit Devices

In a vacuum or gas tube, electrons travel through a much-rarified atmosphere or through a gas. In a solid-state device such as a diode or transistor, electrons travel through a solid—hence the name, "solid state."

TRANSISTORS

Transistors are current-operated devices, whereas tubes are voltage-operated. Computer circuits use both NPN and PNP transistor configurations. Fig. 3-1 shows the contrast in their supply voltages. NPN transistors in a grounded-base arrangement (Fig. 3-1A) have a negative voltage applied to the emitter and a positive

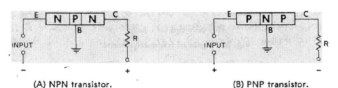

(A) NPN transistor.   (B) PNP transistor.

Fig. 3-1. Supply voltages applied to NPN and PNP transistors.

voltage to the collector. In the PNP transistor, these voltages (or more accurately, current sources) are of opposite polarities (Fig. 3-1B).

Any number of opposite states in a transistor can represent binary 0 and 1. Consider a computer system of logic where 1 is −10 volts and 0 is zero volts. Actually there are many pairs of values for this one-zero combination of binary values—such as pulse and no pulse, positive voltage and negative voltage, or any other such dissimilarities. Three transistor circuits are shown in Fig. 3-2. In Fig. 3-2A an inverter converts a positive pulse into a negative pulse to permit the transition from an NPN to a PNP stage. No inversion occurs in Fig. 3-2B because the output is taken from the emitter load. An inverted follower circuit is shown in Fig. 3-2C.

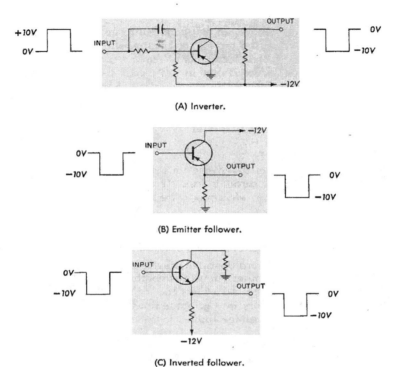

(A) Inverter.

(B) Emitter follower.

(C) Inverted follower.

Fig. 3-2. Types of transistor circuits.

One of the greatest uses of transistors is in multivibrators, of which there are several variations. A multivibrator may be free-running—that is, no input signal is needed to produce an output. A synchronization signal may be introduced, if required, in order to control the frequency of this self-excited oscillator. The flip-flop is another type of multivibrator. It has two stable states; each input pulse switches the circuit to the other state, where it remains until the next pulse. There are also other types, but these are two of the most common in computer circuits.

A free-running oscillator can be used to drive counters or dividers and other computer circuits. For the most precise control of output frequency, crystal oscillators are used with pulse-forming clippers.

DIODES

The use of diodes (both semiconductor and tube) as switching elements in gates is illustrated in Fig. 3-3. This circuit illustrates

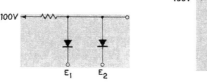

(A) Semiconductor circuit.

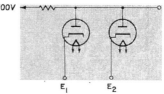

(B) Vacuum-tube circuit.

E_1	E_2	E_0
+2	+2	+2
−5	−5	−5
+2	−5	−5
−5	+2	−5

+2=HIGH
−5=LOW

(C) E_0 produced by each combination of E_1 and E_2.

Fig. 3-3. Diode switching action.

a simple use of a diode pair to make an OR, since any low input will inherently produce a low output. With a positive voltage on both anodes, the diodes conduct because their anodes are more positive than their cathodes. With −5 volts on both cathodes, both diodes again conduct because their anodes are still more positive than their cathodes. However, when E_1 is +2 volts and E_2 is −5 volts there is a change in the circuit. The −5 volts produces a total potential difference of 105 volts (+100 volts on the anode and −5 volts on the cathode), and the diode connected to E_2 conducts. This conduction makes E_0 −5 volts, since in effect the

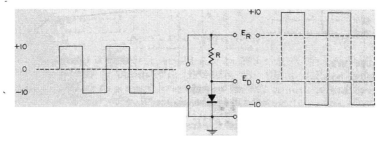

Fig. 3-4. Diode clamping action.

diodes act as short circuits when they conduct. The other diode in each pair now has −5 volts on its anode and +2 volts on its cathode; and since its anode is less negative than its cathode, it cannot conduct.

Diodes have many other uses in computer circuits. Clamps or limiters are used to establish voltage levels beyond which parts

27

of the circuit cannot go. The diode action in Fig. 3-4 will explain the clamping function. Suppose load R is about 10,000 ohms and the diode has a very low forward (conducting) resistance, but has a high back (nonconducting) resistance of about 350,000 ohms. A square wave, as shown, is applied to the resistor and diode in series with two outputs, one across R and the other across the diode. The cathode of the diode is at ground potential. When the input square wave is positive, the diode conducts and its output voltage is in effect zero or ground; but the drop across R is −10 volts. The total effective circuit resistance is just slightly greater than 10,000 ohms.

But when the input voltage is negative, the diode cannot conduct. Almost all of the IR drop is across the diode's 350,000 ohms and there is an output of −10 volts across the diode. During this time there is only a very small output across R. The total effective circuit resistance is 360,000 ohms, or a 35-to-1 ratio between the voltage of the diode and the voltage across R.

Two clamp circuits are shown in Fig. 3-5; Fig. 3-5A is an upper clamp and Fig. 3-5B a lower clamp. In Fig. 3-5A the cathode of

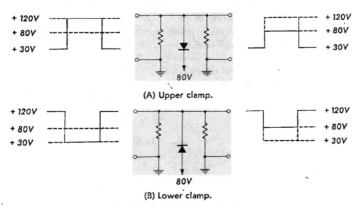

(A) Upper clamp.

(B) Lower clamp.

Fig. 3-5. Diode clamping circuits.

the diode goes to 80 volts and the input swings 90 volts, from +30 to +120 volts. As the input voltage rises to 80 volts, the output voltage follows it exactly, since the diode is not conducting. But as soon as the input rises above 80 volts, its anode becomes more positive than its cathode, and the diode conducts. This action "clamps" the output to +80 volts and prevents it from rising above this value. When the input square wave drops below 80 volts, the output voltage follows as before.

In the lower clamp in Fig. 3-5B, the action is reversed. Here the diode's anode goes to 80 volts. The input is a negative-going square wave that swings from +120 to +30 volts. When the input goes from 120 to 80 volts, the output follows, since the diode is not conducting. As soon as the cathode drops below 80 volts, it is now less positive than the anode, and the diode conducts. This action clamps the output so that it cannot drop below 80 volts.

A double clamp is shown on the vacuum-tube amplifier in Fig. 3-6. When the grid signal cuts off the tube, M1 conducts and prevents the output (plate voltage) from rising above 150 volts. (Nor-

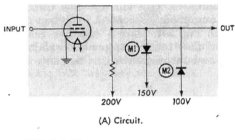

(A) Circuit.

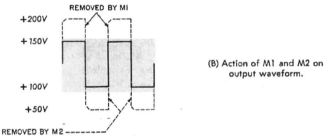

(B) Action of M1 and M2 on output waveform.

Fig. 3-6. A double-clamp circuit.

mally, without a clamp it would rise to 200 volts.) At saturation, when the tube is conducting heavily, the plate voltage would ordinarily drop to a very low value; but M2 conducts and limits this value to 100 volts. Thus, for this set of conditions the output is a square wave swinging only from +100 to +150 volts, in spite of a large driving signal.

PHOTOELECTRIC COMPONENTS

Photoelectric devices in the computer read punched paper tapes and convert these readings from light into electrical power for a host of applications.

The three types of photoelectric devices are photoconductive or photosensitive (those which change their resistance), photoemissive (those which emit electrons), and photovoltaic (those which generate a voltage). All of these devices are used for inputs in computer systems.

The most important are the semiconductor photoconductive devices, which are thin layers of selenium, silicon, cadmium sulfide, lead sulfide, lead selenide, etc., sealed in glass. A simple circuit arrangement has a voltage impressed across the cell, and a series resistor. With no light falling on the cell, it has a high resistance and thus limits the current flow. But when light strikes the semiconductor material of the cell, its resistance decreases and the series current increases. This current flow through the load resistance can be amplified for control. Another possible arrangement is shown in Fig. 3-7. Here a sensitive relay, which closes when the current flow increases, has been added to the circuit, so that a larger amount of power can be controlled through the relay contacts.

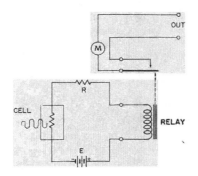

Fig. 3-7. A photocell circuit.

In addition to photoconductive cells, light-sensitive semiconductor diodes called photodiodes are used. Light, falling on the PN junction, decreases the resistance to the current flow established by a DC voltage across the diode. This current flow varies with the incident light, and the output is applied to a following control amplifier. Such circuits are often used by the computer to translate light impulses into signals. For example, punched cards or tapes have a series of holes or slots, each representing a number or other data. By shining lights through the holes, it is possible for photoelectric devices to detect the proper cards and reject all others.

The phototransistor is similar in action to the photodiode. It is a light-sensitive transistor such as a special PNP germanium alloy junction. These light-controlled miniature devices have a wide variety of industrial and military applications where light is utilized to actuate electronic equipment, such as punched card and tape readouts in computer systems. The primary advantages of phototransistors over other photosensitive devices are their small size, low power consumption, head-on construction, good light sensitivity, and superior response to high-frequency chopped light.

Phototransistors are sometimes called *light tetrodes* because carriers can be injected into the base by a signal voltage applied to the base lead (as with any other transistor), or by light energy falling on the base. These two conditions may occur together as well as separately.

OTHER SEMICONDUCTORS

Transistors and diodes are quite important circuit elements in computers. They can act as flip-flops, switches, amplifiers, and other circuit blocks; but they are only one of a family of semiconductors.

Solid-state devices make possible the small packaged circuits used in the newer, desk-sized computers. Some of the more recent circuit developments are integrated packages containing several circuit functions such as inductance, capacitance, resistance, and amplification in a single element. Silicon or germanium can be used for several circuit elements, and already demonstrated is a complete solid-state multivibrator the size of a match head! For example, a resistor is made by using two ohmic (nonrectifying) contacts to the silicon or germanium material; transistors and diodes, by using the diffused-base technique; and capacitors, by using a large-area junction.

Tunnel (Esaki) diodes offer great promise in computer switching circuits. These highly doped PN junctions have a negative-resistance characteristic curve—as the forward voltage increases, the current rises to a very high value and then dips. This negative conductance gives the tunnel diode a great potential in computer circuits.

The *unijunction transistor* is another new semiconductor component. Originally called a double-base diode, it differs in both construction and operation from the conventional transistor. In contrast to the latter, the unijunction transistor has open-circuit, stable negative-resistance characteristics. Because of this it is useful primarily in switching and oscillator circuits. In addition, it has the unique ability to sense voltage levels and temperature variations; or by various circuit modifications, it can be made insensitive to them. These devices are particularly useful as relaxation oscillators, sawtooth and pulse generators, pulse-rate modulators, pulse amplifiers, multivibrators, flip-flops, and delay circuits. Because of its high peak current rating of 2 amperes, the unijunction transistor can do the work of two conventional

31

transistors in medium-power switching and in oscillator applications. In certain voltage-sensing and locking circuits, one unijunction transistor can replace as many as five conventional transistors!

The unijunction transistor can be operated in a number of different circuit configurations, so that any one of the three terminals will serve as a signal input or load output.

Because the switching properties of the *four-layer transistor diode* closely approach those of the ideal switch, it is finding numerous applications in computers. Some of these include pulse generators and amplifiers, oscillators, alarm circuits, ring counters, switching, and magnetic core driving. It also provides the unusual combination of power-handling ability and fast switching.

The four-layer diode often replaces relays, thyratrons, gas diodes, and switching transistors. Before switching, its reverse-biased junction acts as a capacitor. It is necessary, in the course of switching, to charge this capacitor as well as to inject current carriers into it. The energy required must be furnished either by the trigger pulse, or by circuit elements provided for this purpose.

This transistor-like device functions as a semiconductor switch by virtue of its two states. One is an open-circuit condition, where it acts as a large resistance—in the 10- to 1,000-megohm range. The other is a closed, or low-resistance, state, where it acts almost like a short circuit. This two-terminal device can be considered a PNP and NPN transistor tied together as in Fig. 3-8. At the proper applied voltage, the center junction breaks down and current flows. Hence the device can function as a switch.

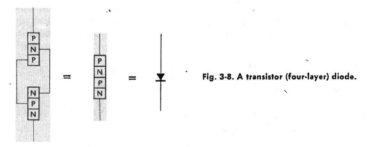

Fig. 3-8. A transistor (four-layer) diode.

In its "off" condition, the transistor diode can be considered a capacitance and a large resistance in parallel. The value of this capacitance, which is similar to the collector capacitance of a normal transistor, depends on the voltage across the diode. In the "on" condition, the resistance is so low that capacitive effects can be ignored.

32

In its "off" condition, the device will pass a capacitive current in response to a sharply rising voltage wave. If this wave rises fast enough, switching will occur below the DC switching voltage.

A limiting resistor or other load impedance is placed in series with the transistor diode to prevent it from passing excessive current in the "on" state. Since its resistance decreases with increasing current (to less than 1 ohm at high pulse currents), the transistor diode can be destroyed unless the load current is limited.

MAGNETICS

Magnetism is very useful for data storage, because it remains after the current source that created it is gone. Magnetic materials are used in modern digital computers as both memory and logical devices. These materials include a group known as ferrites, which are ceramic-like magnetic substances made from oxides of iron, cobalt, nickel, aluminum, magnesium, and manganese. Although metallic and magnetic, they are nonconductors and hence their hysteresis loss is very low. The electrons of the ferrite material are affected by external magnetic fields, however.

Tape-wound cores, which are bobbins with layers of thin magnetic materials, are used in magnetic shift registers. The cores are tape-wound to reduce their losses.

Core Memories

Ferrites act as a memory, or storage, for data in digital computers and control devices. A large number of interconnected magnetic cores form the heart of the memory unit.

The memory has hundreds of locations, or addresses, all of which can store information until needed. Each location can be described and located, so that its information can be obtained, or else the location of new storages to which it was sent can be described. Reading out the information from the memory may destroy the data; or the same information can be regenerated and referred to as often as needed, depending on the program. In certain computers, all the information needed for the solution to a problem may be stored in the memory, including all the steps of the program. In this way, once the proper information has been placed in the memory, the computer is independent of all outside devices until it reaches a solution. Then the final results are stored until called for through the output device.

Fig. 3-9 shows a magnetic memory toroid. If current passes through the threading wire as in Fig. 3-9A, the magnetic field will be clockwise; and an opposite current will produce the counterclockwise magnetic field in Fig. 3-9B. Thus, a magnetic core has two stable states, corresponding to 0 and 1. To sense or

33

read out, the core has another winding as shown in Fig. 3-9C. If the core is in the "clear" position, there will be *no* output when a pulse is passed through this winding; but there *will* be an output when the core is in the "set" position.

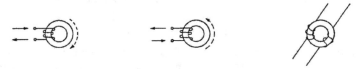

(A) Clockwise magnetic field.

(B) Counterclockwise magnetic field.

(C) Addition of readout winding.

Fig. 3-9. Ferrite cores.

Part of a memory core array is shown in Fig. 3-10. Two sets of wires, called *write lines,* give and take information from each core. One set is vertical and the other is horizontal. A current of I amperes is required to set a core in order to store a 1. Half of this current ($\frac{1}{2}$I) is sent through the vertical write line, which goes through four cores; and the other half is sent through the horizontal write line, which likewise goes through four cores. But since only a single core is threaded by both lines (at their inter-

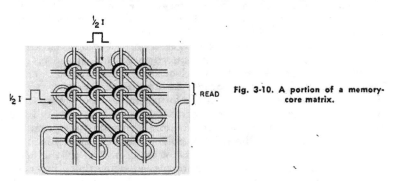

Fig. 3-10. A portion of a memory-core matrix.

section), this core receives $\frac{1}{2}$I from each line, or the full I amperes. Only this core receives enough current to change it from one state to another; all others with a write current receive only $\frac{1}{2}$I.

A third wire, the read line, goes through all cores; since only one core is switched at a time, this change of flux appears in the read line. To determine the state of a selected core, it is pulsed with a 1. If it already has a 1 in it, there will be *no* output from the read wiring; but if it has a 0, there *will* be an output.

34

Magnetic Tapes

Magnetic tapes, used on all but the earliest computers, contain the program data (list of instructions that control the computer step by step). Large amounts of such data can be stored in tape bins, and in this way a library of programs developed for future use. The programmer selects and feeds the appropriate tapes to the input system, and the computer slavishly follows the recorded instructions until the program is completed (a solution is reached).

An oil refinery, for example, has dozens or even hundreds of storage tanks, and keeping track of the gallonage in each could be a problem. This is one of the computer's easier tasks. An automatic system reads the level in each tank. This reading is fed into the computer, which looks up a table (stored on tape) for that tank and—from the tape—measures, calculates, and records its exact gallonage to provide an automatic perpetual inventory.

Banks, swamped under bales of paperwork, have found some relief in automation. Each account is kept on tape, and deposits or withdrawals can be quickly brought up-to-date and the latest balance immediately obtained. One master set of tapes can serve any number of branch offices.

Department stores are also using magnetic tape in data-processing systems to provide management, in minutes or hours, with complete sales data and inventories which by other methods would take several days or even weeks.

In normal data-handling terminology, each 1 in a pulse train is represented by a pulse and each 0 by the absence of a pulse.

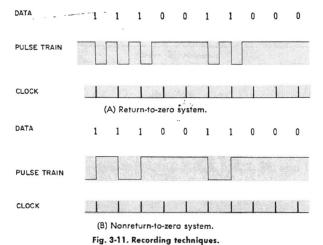

(A) Return-to-zero system.

(B) Nonreturn-to-zero system.

Fig. 3-11. Recording techniques.

35

This is known as the "return-to-zero" method of data representation—the signal always returns to base level after each pulse in order to represent a 1, as in Fig. 3-11A.

There are other methods of representing data, in which the signal does not always return to the base level. In one such method (known for obvious reasons as the "non-return-to-zero" system), the signal remains at one of two levels as shown in Fig. 3-11B. The only time this level changes is when the data appears as a 1; a 0 represents no change.

In magnetic recording, the density with which the pulses can be packed on the tape is extremely important, since the speed of the tape or drum is mechanically limited. With a "non-return-to-zero" recording it is possible to pack them more densely because the flux pattern changes only when a pulse appears. Also, there is a maximum of one change per "bit" of information recorded on the tape.

Magnetic Drums

One technique for mass storage is the magnetic drum, which is a group of magnetic rings or tracks around a revolving drum. Magnetic recording and playback are much the same as with a tape, except the drum heads do not contact the magnetized surface, but are situated just above the magnetic area.

Magnetic drums and other types of magnetic storage are discussed further in a later chapter on storage.

CHAPTER 4

Numbers
for Computers

Computers use the binary numbering system based on a count of 2. We, of course, are most familiar with our decimal system, based on acount of 10; but there are other equally valid numbering systems using other bases. The only reason they seem strange or difficult is that we are so used to thinking in terms of the base 10. Some of the other systems are the binary, using the base 2; the bi-quinary, using 10 by pairs; and Roman numerals. Our decimal system is used by most desk calculators, Roman numerals have their own special purposes, and the bi-quinary system is the basis of the abacus.

NUMBERING SYSTEMS

The decimal system bears closer examination. Take the digits 2 3 for example. In the decimal system, they mean 2 tens and 3 ones. To the base 5, however, 23 means 2 fives and 3 ones, or 13 in the decimal system. And using the base 8, 23 is 2 eights

Table 4-1. Counting from decimal 1 to 10 in three numbering systems.

Base	Order of Numbers									
10	1	2	3	4	5	6	7	8	9	10
8	1	2	3	4	5	6	7	10	11	12
5	1	2	3	4	10	11	12	13	14	20

and 3 ones, or decimal 19. Table 4-1 gives the decimal numbers 1 through 10 and their equivalents using the base 8 and the base 5. The counting in the decimal system is the familiar 1, 2, 3, 4, 5, 6, 7, 8, 9, 10. To the base 8 it is 1, 2, 3, 4, 5, 6, 7, 10; and to the base 5 it is 1, 2, 3, 4, 10.

Because we use decimal numbers so often, we tend to forget they are not found in all applications. For instance, when we see VIII, what number comes to mind? In the decimal system, 5 and 3 in the number 53 mean 5 tens and 3 ones. But Roman numeral VIII is 1 five and 3 ones, or 8 in our decimal system.

Any numbering system is composed of digits which have arbitrary, specific values. After all numbers in sequence have been used up in the first position, a second position is added, starting with the first number; when the second position is filled, a third position is added, etc. For example, in the system of A B C in

Table 4-2. ABC numbering system.

Decimal	ABC	Decimal	ABC	Decimal	ABC
1	A	14	AAB	27	BBC
2	B	15	AAC	28	BCA
3	C	16	ABA	29	BCB
4	AA	17	ABB	30	BCC
5	AB	18	ABC	31	CAA
6	AC	19	ACA	32	CAB
7	BA	20	ACB	33	CAC
8	BB	21	ACC	34	CBA
9	BC	22	BAA	35	CBB
10	CA	23	BAB	36	CBC
11	CB	24	BAC	37	CCA
12	CC	25	BBA	38	CCB
13	AAA	26	BBB	39	CCC

Table 4-2, A is 1, AC is 6, AAB is 14, BBC is 27, and CCB is 38 in our decimal system. Why is CCB equal to 38? Because here the first C at the left means 3 nines, the second C means 3 threes, and the B means 2 ones $(27 + 9 + 2 = 38)$. In the same manner CBA is 34, or $27 + 6 + 1$.

Our everyday numbering system is based on 10, and any number can be written as the sum of a series of numbers, each a power of 10, as shown in Fig. 4-1A. Another way of showing

$$352 = \begin{cases} 300 \\ 50 \\ 2 \\ \overline{352} \end{cases}$$

$$4167 = \begin{cases} 4000 \\ 100 \\ 60 \\ 7 \\ \overline{4167} \end{cases}$$

$$50{,}213 = \begin{cases} 50000 \\ 200 \\ 10 \\ 3 \\ \overline{50213} \end{cases}$$

(A) As a sum of a series of numbers.

10^4 (10,000)	10^3 (1,000)	10^2 (100)	10^1 (10)	10^0 (1)
		3	5	2
	4	1	6	7
5	0	2	1	3

(B) As a series of powers of ten.

Fig. 4-1. Decimal notation.

this is by making columns for each power of 10 and writing the digits in their proper places, as shown in Fig. 4-1B. Each column, reading from right to left, increases by 1 in the power of 10; for example, 4167 is, $4(1000) + 1(100) + 6(10) + 7(1)$. So, for mechanization and subsequent use in an adding machine or computer, the decimal system of numbering to the base 10 requires ten entirely different and recognizable states for each digit.

Mathematically, any numbering system requires m states, where m is the base. Since most vacuum tubes or transistors have only two stable states which are *dependable*, 10 separate devices are needed, one for each digit. This is more clearly indicated in Fig. 4-2, where each transistor is either "on" or "off."

	10^3	10^2	10^1	10^0
0	—	—	—	—
1	—	—	—	—
2	ON	—	—	—
3	—	—	—	—
4	—	ON	—	—
5	—	—	—	—
6	—	—	ON	—
7	—	—	—	—
8	—	—	—	—
9	—	—	—	ON

Fig. 4-2. Light arrangement indicating the number 2469.

But first it would be wise to review the system of powers. Any number can be written as a power series, the number 2469_{10} being expressed as:

$$2469 = 2000 + 400 + 60 + 9$$
$$= 2(10^3) + 4(10^2) + 6(10^1) + 9(10^0)$$

Thus, 2469_{10} will appear as shown in Fig. 4-2. There are four sets of ten transistor indicators. In each set one light is on, indicating the digit in that column. Hence, 40 transistor indicators

Table 4-3. Counting to the base 5.

	Base 5			Base 5	
Decimal	5^1	5^0	Decimal	5^1	5^0
1	0	1	9	1	4
2	0	2	10	2	0
3	0	3	11	2	1
4	0	4	12	2	2
5	1	0	13	2	3
6	1	1	14	2	4
7	1	2	15	3	0
8	1	3			

are needed in order to represent a four-digit number. Each digit has a string from 0 to 9, and only one transistor can be on at any one time—a tremendous waste of space and cost since so many idle transistors must be accommodated.

39

Any number can be expressed as a power series, as was shown for 2469. Moreover, any base can be used to express a given number, in place of our customary 10. Let the base be 5, as an example: a count from decimal 0 to 15, to the base 5, would be as in Table 4-3. Representing 2469_{10} to the base 5 would thus require only half as many transistors.

$$2469_{10} = 34,334_5$$
$$34,334_5 = 3(5^4) + 4(5^3) + 3(5^2) + 3(5^1) + 4(5^0)$$
$$2469_{10} = 1875 + 500 + 75 + 15 + 4$$

This number indication can be seen from Fig. 4-3, a visual representation of the number 34,334 to the base 5. Other numbering systems also exist and, for some applications, are more useful than the decimal system. One of these is the binary system.

	5^4	5^3	5^2	5^1	5^0
0	—	—	—	—	—
1	—	—	—	—	—
2	—	—	—	—	—
3	ON	—	ON	ON	—
4	—	ON	—	—	ON

Fig. 4-3. Light arrangement indicating the number 34334 to the base 5.

BINARY NOTATION

Switches for industrial control systems operate on a two-valued system such as "on-off" or "open-closed." Vacuum tubes and transistors in digital computers also operate like simple switches to either *permit* or *prevent* current flow. Since they have but two states, these switching devices cannot easily be used for representing the decimal system.

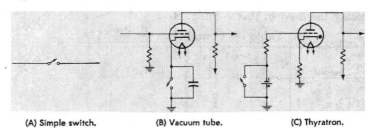

(A) Simple switch.   (B) Vacuum tube.   (C) Thyratron.

Fig. 4-4. Three types of switching circuits.

Some examples of switches are illustrated in Fig. 4-4. The simple two-position switch in Fig. 4-4A has two states, open and closed; so it can be used as a binary device. Others can be tubes. The vacuum tube in Fig. 4-4B will conduct or will be cut off, depending on the position of the switch in series with the cathode.

40

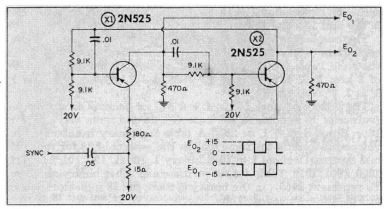

Fig. 4-5. A transistor multivibrator circuit.

A gas-filled tube (Fig. 4-4C) can also be used. It will conduct only when the switch shorts the bias. The switch and the tubes are all two-state devices.

A transistor multivibrator is shown in Fig. 4-5. The string of pulses comprising the free-running output can be considered a

Table 4-4. Binary numbers.

Decimal Value	2^5 (32)	2^4 (16)	2^3 (8)	2^2 (4)	2^1 (2)	2^0 (1)
	BINARY REPRESENTATION					
0	0	0	0	0	0	0
1	0	0	0	0	0	1
2	0	0	0	0	1	0
3	0	0	0	0	1	1
4	0	0	0	1	0	0
5	0	0	0	1	0	1
6	0	0	0	1	1	0
7	0	0	0	1	1	1
8	0	0	1	0	0	0
9	0	0	1	0	0	1
10	0	0	1	0	1	0
12	0	0	1	1	0	0
14	0	0	1	1	1	0
16	0	1	0	0	0	0
18	0	1	0	0	1	0
20	0	1	0	1	0	0
23	0	1	0	1	1	1
27	0	1	1	0	1	1
31	0	1	1	1	1	1
37	1	0	0	1	0	1
43	1	0	1	0	1	1
48	1	1	0	0	0	0
50	1	1	0	0	1	0
57	1	1	1	0	0	1
63	1	1	1	1	1	1

series of binary digits such as 0, 1, 0, 1, etc., where zero volts is a 0 and 15 volts (either positive or negative) is a 1.

The numbering system most easily adaptable for use in digital computers is the binary based on successive powers of 2, as shown in Table 4-4. Only two digits are used, 1 and 0. The powers of 2 are: 1, 2, 4, 8, 16, and 32. Just as 10^0 is 1, so 2^0 is also 1; 2^1 is 2, 2^2 is 4, etc.

The binary number 101 is $4 + 0 + 1$ or decimal 5, written 5_{10} (subscript 10 denotes to the base 10). In the same way 10111 is $16 + 0 + 4 + 2 + 1$, or 23_{10}. A table for binary numbers is developed in exactly the same way as the powers of 10 for the decimal system. Decimal 1 to 10 is binary 1, 10, 11, 100, 101, 110, 111, 1000, 1001, 1010. Table 4-4 shows these and other binary numbers. To represent 2469_{10} in the binary system, the 12 indicators shown in Fig. 4-6 are needed. Thus,

$$2048 + 256 + 128 + 32 + 4 + 1 = 2469_{10},$$
and
$$100110100101_2 = 2469_{10}.$$

To express a binary digit (called a *bit* from *binary digit*), only one indicator is needed—"on" represents a *1*, and "off" a *0*. In the computer the input data is converted to binary, usually in a

Power	2^{11}	2^{10}	2^9	2^8	2^7	2^6	2^5	2^4	2^3	2^2	2^1	2^0
Decimal Value	2048	1024	512	256	128	64	32	16	8	4	2	1
Binary	1	0	0	1	1	0	1	0	0	1	0	1

Fig. 4-6. Converting the decimal number 2469 to a binary number.

coded system. The computations are made using the binary system, and output data is converted from binary back to decimal.

All the circuit devices in Chapters 2 and 3 act as binary devices. The binary system not only can represent decimal numbers but, by coding, it can be made to represent letters of the alphabet as well.

CHAPTER 5

Arithmetic Operations

One of the major advantages of the binary numbering system is the ease with which arithmetic problems can be solved in a digital computer. Very few rules, and no tables, are required to solve any addition, subtraction, multiplication, or division problem. The over-all problem is first broken down into a series of individual operations.

ADDITION

Addition has only four rules:

0	0	1	1
0	1	0	1
0	1	1	10

Here 1 plus 1 is 10 (pronounced "one-oh") because binary 10 is decimal 2. This is the same as saying that decimal 1 plus 1 is 2.

Following these rules, it is possible to add any two binary numbers directly. For example, to add decimal 12 and 5:

$$
\begin{array}{rl}
12 & \text{is the same as binary} \quad 1100 \\
5 & \text{is the same as binary} \quad \underline{101} \\
\hline
17 & \text{is the same as binary} \quad 10001
\end{array}
$$

To add 01011 and 00110:

Binary	Decimal
01011	11
00110	6
10001	17

In binary addition there is the problem of the carry, as when $1 + 1 = 10$ — that is, 0 plus carry 1. This can be seen from the following, where 111101 is added to 10110:

43

(A)	111101
(B)	10110
(C)	101011
(D)	1 1
(E)	1010011

The first step is to add the two (A and B) to get the partial sum (C). Line D shows the two carries resulting from the 1 + 1 sums. Adding partial sum C, and the carries D, produces the final sum E, or 1010011.

A digital computer is actually a much expanded version of an adding machine, doing electronically what the adding machine accomplishes through a mechanical system of gears, etc. Basically, the operation of the two is the same, for purposes of illustration.

A digital computer, once given its orders by the operator, stores them in its memory and then recalls each order one by one until the solution is reached. Although its operation is superhumanly fast, a computer requires instructions for each step. It can do only what it is told; having a limited memory and no imagination, it cannot think as humans do.

Each computer operation is determined by a series of instructions which direct the flow of information, as shown in Fig. 5-1. Each block represents a *register,* one of a group of series-con-

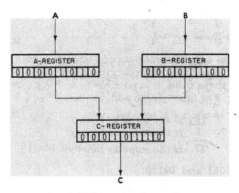

Fig. 5-1. Addition using three registers.

nected circuits which can store ("remember") a number and make it perform a certain operation. Suppose the computer's instructions are: "Add A to B and place in C." This means the number stored in register A is to be added to the number in register B, and the sum then placed in register C. Assuming

44

numbers are already in registers A and B, the computer automatically does the following steps:

1. Clears register C by removing any information there. This it does by inserting a 0 in each stage of C.
2. Transfers to C the number stored in A (1010). C is connected to A, stage by stage. In this program the computer is also told not to "forget" the 1010, but to store it in A for later use. (1010 happens to be the constant in this specific program.) C and A both now have the same number.
3. Adds the number in B (1100) to the number in C (1010), following the rules of binary addition discussed earlier. In this program the computer is also told to keep B's memory a total blank in order to make room for the next variable.
4. Final conditions: Register A still has the original number stored, and will continue to do so until cleared; B is cleared (in this program) by the addition to C; and C now contains the sum.

SUBTRACTION

Subtraction of binary numbers is done in two ways. One is by direct subtraction:

$$\begin{array}{r} 101101 \\ -1011 \\ \hline 100010 \end{array}$$

Note that to subtract 1 from 0, it is necessary to borrow 1, making 1 from 10, or 1.

Complements also provide a means of subtraction. In our decimal system the 10's complement is the difference between 10 and a given number—hence, the complement of 7 is 3. By the same token, the 9's complement is the difference between 9 and a given number, the complement of 7 being 2.

By *addition* of complements, it is possible to perform subtraction. First, here is how subtraction is normally done in the decimal system:

$$\begin{array}{r} 7 \\ -3 \\ \hline 4 \end{array}$$

To subtract, using the 10's complement system:

$$\begin{array}{r} 7 \\ +7 \\ \hline 14 \end{array} \quad \text{(the 10's complement of 3; } 10-3=7)$$

Drop the extra first digit (which occurs because of the complement), giving the remainder, 4.

Using the 9's complement system:

$$7$$
$$\underline{+6} \quad \text{(the 9's complement of 3: } 9-3=6\text{)}$$
$$13$$

Here, however, the extra 1 is not dropped, but is *added* to the 3 (the mathematical reason is beyond the scope of this discussion), giving the same answer, 4. This adding of the extra 1, known as *end-around carry*, is a vital step in computer subtraction, as we shall soon see.

In the binary system there are only two digits, 1 and 0; so, of course, there can be only two complements. To find the 1's complement of 1, subtract 1 from 1, giving 0 $(1-1=0)$. Again, to find the 1's complement of 0, subtract it from 1, giving 1 $(1-0=1)$. In other words, to find the complement of a binary number, change all 1's to 0's and all 0's to 1's. Thus, the complement of 1011 is 0100.

But first, to subtract binary numbers directly:

$$1101$$
$$\underline{-1011}$$
$$0010$$

And since the complement of 1011 is 0100, subtraction is also possible by adding complements:

$$1101$$
$$\underline{+0100}$$
$$10001$$
$$\llcorner\!\!\rightarrow 1 \quad \text{(end-around carry)}$$
$$\overline{0010}$$

This complement technique is important because of the circuit design of a digital computer. If the number is held in a register which is a series of flip-flops, complementing requires a change of state for each flip-flop.

0	0	1	1	
0	1	0	1	ADDITION
0	1	1	10	
0	0	1	1	
0	1	0	1	MULTIPLICATION
0	0	0	1	

Fig. 5-2. Binary rules of arithmetic.

MULTIPLICATION

For multiplication there are four rules, which can be reduced to two. As shown in Fig. 5-2, $1 \times 1 = 1$, and all other combinations are zero. For example, to multiply 1011 by 0101:

Binary	Decimal
1011	11
0101	×5
1011	55
1011	
110111	

To multiply decimal 12 and 5:

1100	12
101	×5
1100	60
11000	
111100	

In binary multiplication there are no tables, no carries (except in adding partial products), and every product is equal to 0 except 1×1, which is 1. Multiplication is a series of additions, just as multiplying 14 by 8 in the decimal system is the same as adding 14 eight times. Binary 10101 is multiplied by 101 as follows:

$$10101$$
$$\underline{101}$$
$$10101$$
$$0$$
$$\underline{10101}$$
$$1101001$$

Multiplication is thus a series of shifts and additions, as in the decimal system. With 101 as the multiplier, each 1 is a shift left and an addition, and each 0 is a shift but *no* addition.

For example, to multiply 100101 by 101:

100101	
101	
100101	
00000	(shift left, no add)
100101	(shift left and add)
10111001	(sum)

For every 1 in the multiplier (101), the multiplicand (100101) is moved one place to the left and added. For every 0 in 101, there is one shift but no addition.

Multiplication or division as a series of shifts can be seen in Fig. 5-3. The original number in the register is A, or 1010100. If A is shifted left one place—a multiplication by 2—the result appears as in B. The second shift left, at C, results in 101010000, or 4 times A. The shift right is a division by 2, as in D; two shifts right (A divided by 4) produces a second division by 2, as in E.

A	0	0	1	0	1	0	1	0	0	
			√	SHIFT LEFT						
B	0	1	0	1	0	1	0	0	0	
	√	SHIFT LEFT								
C	1	0	1	0	1	0	0	0	0	
A	0	0	1	0	1	0	1	0	0	
					√	SHIFT RIGHT				
D	0	0	0	1	0	1	0	1	0	
						√	SHIFT RIGHT			
E	0	0	0	0	1	0	1	0	1	

Fig. 5-3. Multiplication and division as a series of shifts.

To repeat, shifting left is a form of multiplication and shifting right is division. Starting with 101100, a shift left is 1011000 which is twice 101100; and dividing by 2 is a shift right, or 10110.

One more example: Starting with 101100 (decimal 44), a shift left is 1011000 (decimal 88); and a shift right is 10110 (decimal 22). This is exactly like operating with decimal numbers. Taking 347.036 a shift left would be 3470.36, which is ten times 347.036; and a shift right would be 34.7036, which is one-tenth of 347.036.

DIVISION

Division can also be done in the usual way, by long division. The divisor is subtracted from the dividend and a 1 placed in the quotient. If the divisor cannot be subtracted, a 0 is placed in the quotient. As an example:

$$
\begin{array}{r}
10101 \\
101\overline{)1101010} \\
101 \\
\hline
110 \\
101 \\
\hline
110 \\
101 \\
\hline
1
\end{array}
$$

Thus, 101 goes into 1101010   10101 times with a remainder of 1.

OCTAL NUMBERING

Like any machine, the computer is prone to error. So its operation must occasionally be checked, step by step, by a human operator. For this purpose the decimal numbering system is inadequate, because the computer can use only the binary system. But there are no mechanical calculators which operate directly from the binary system, and it would be a long and tedious task by hand. Thus, we find that the octal system of numbering to the base 8 is used. Conversion from octal to decimal and vice versa is relatively simple. Table 5-1 gives the binary equivalents of octal 0 through 7. (Note that they are the same as decimal 0 through 7.)

Table 5-1. Binary triplets.

Octal (Decimal)	Binary Triplet		
0	0	0	0
1	0	0	1
2	0	1	0
3	0	1	1
4	1	0	0
5	1	0	1
6	1	1	0
7	1	1	1

Since any octal number can be written with a binary triplet (group of 3 digits), conversion from a binary to an octal number is simple and direct. The binary number is broken down into groups of three digits, and each group is then converted to its octal number. (Where necessary, zeros are added in front of the number to make groups of threes.) For example, to convert 1011 to an octal number:

$$001011$$

$$1 \quad 3$$

Thus, binary 1011 is octal 13. Now that we know how to convert from binary to octal, let's see how the latter is used to check the accuracy of a computer:

$$
\begin{array}{lll}
111 & \text{is octal} & 7 \\
+010 & \text{is octal} & +2 \\
\hline
001001 & \text{is octal} & 11 \\
\end{array}
$$

$$1 \quad 1$$

The two answers check. One more example:

$$\begin{array}{ll}
\dot{1}01 & \text{is octal} \quad 5 \\
+110 & \text{is octal} \quad +6 \\
\hline
001011 & \text{is octal} \quad 13 \\
1 \quad 3 &
\end{array}$$

As we said before, conversion from binary to decimal or vice versa, although possible, is not convenient; the octal system, however, is directly related to the binary system and hence easier to work with.

NUMBERING CODES

A combination of decimal and binary is often used, such as the binary-coded decimal in Table 5-2. Each decimal digit is

Table 5-2. Binary-coded decimals.

Decimal	Binary-Coded Decimal
0	0000
1	0001
2	0010
3	0011
4	0100
5	0101
6	0110
7	0111
8	1000
9	1001

coded. For example, 18 in pure binary is 10010; but in binary-coded decimal it is 00011000. In this way it is possible to convert each digit individually, rather than having to convert the entire number. This ease of conversion is obviously the advantage of the binary-coded decimal.

Another code in frequent use is the "excess-3," in which each binary number is represented as three more than its actual value. This permits direct subtraction using complements.

Other codes are also employed. One is the gray, or reflected, binary, in which each change from one number to the next in sequence requires only a change in one bit (binary digit). Another is the alpha-numeric code, in which binary numbers are also used to represent letters, punctuation marks, and other symbols. For example, A is 010011, ! is 011110, etc.

CHAPTER 6

Symbolic Logic

Digital computers are made up of various types of simple circuits, arranged and grouped according to the rules of symbolic logic. Hence, to understand how a circuit operates and what it does, it is necessary to know a little about logic.

INTRODUCTION TO LOGIC

Logic is the science of establishing the validity of thought or reason, so that what is true in one statement will be true in all equivalent statements. Truths can be classified into four statements, called *propositions:*

1. All A is B. ("All dogs are animals.")
2. Some A is B. ("Some dogs are dachshunds.")
3. No A is B. ("No dogs are birds.")
4. Some A is not B. ("Some dogs are not dachshunds.")

These four absurdly simple examples are recognized truths. Working from them, *and from them alone,* it is possible to deduce a number of further truths. For example, let us change No. 1 into Nos. 2, 3, and 4, and see which are true and which are obviously false.

1. All dogs are animals.
2. Some dogs are animals.
3. No dogs are animals.
4. Some dogs are not animals.

Assuming No. 1 is true, then No. 2 is obviously true *always;* but Nos. 3 and 4 are obviously false *always.* Try these truisms yourself with, say, "all bananas are fruits," or any other known truth.

Many other deductions can be made from these four statements. Interested readers are referred to any textbook on logic for the complete list.

Propositions, if true, can be put together to form a *syllogism:* If it is true that:

All dogs are animals, and that
Rover is a dog; then one can deduce without a doubt that
Rover is an animal.

Establishing the validity of statements 1 and 2 is another matter; this is the job of inductive reasoning, which will not be covered here. But when 1 and 2 are true in this syllogism, the conclusion is valid. Using symbols as we did in the beginning:

All D are A.

R is a D.

∴R is an A

For "is" or "are" it is possible to substitute its algebraic equivalent, the equal sign. ("All D equals A" means "all D are A.")

$$D = A$$
$$R = D$$
$$∴R = A$$

This is symbolic algebra in its crudest form.

Symbolic logic traces its first real beginning to the works of Gottfried W. Leibniz (1646-1716), who tried to create "a general method in which all truths of reason would be reduced to a kind of calculation"; and to Augustus de Morgan (1806-1876). Both attempted to convert logic into algebraic equations. But the founder of symbolic logic was George Boole (1815-1864), who gave the world a form of logic now known as Boolean algebra.

A number of works on mathematical logic had appeared after this, but it was not until 1938 that the possibility of teaming up logic and mechanics was recognized. Claude E. Shannon, then a student at the Massachusetts Institute of Technology, in his now classic paper "A Symbolic Analysis of Relay and Switching Circuits" (*Transactions of the A.I.E.E.* Vol 57, 1938) pointed out: " . . . any circuit is represented by a set of equations, the terms of the equation corresponding to the various relays and switches in the circuit. . . . Our notation is taken chiefly from symbolic logic."

The basic and simple ideas of logic outlined by Boole, Shannon, and their predecessors provide the foundation for many of the circuit applications in digital computers. But logical design is not limited to this area alone. The same principles have a direct bearing on, and an increasing importance in, control circuits for other electronic devices, such as those for automatic control of manufacturing processes. Wherever relays, transistors, or vacuum tubes are used for control, logic will be an aid in understanding circuit operation, just as for computers.

RULES OF CIRCUIT LOGIC

Relay circuits make a convenient starting point in the study of circuit logic, because their principles are applicable to those of transistor or vacuum-tube circuits as well. Circuit symbolism is taken from formal logic, which begins with the fundamental idea that a statement is either true or false—it can be nothing else. Correspondingly, a relay is either open or closed.

In logic, two connectives—AND and OR—express the relationships between two statements. OR means either class A or class B individually, or both class A and class B together. For example, the class "females" and the class "piano players" can be thought of individually, or the two can be thought of as two groups—say, in two separate rooms, or mixed together in one large room. The circuit representation of OR is relays in parallel.

The other connective, AND, is the class of "females" who are "piano players"; in other words the two classes, when thought of in the AND sense, are inseparable. To return to our room analogy,

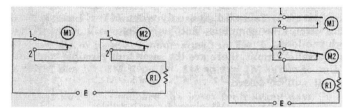

(A) AND (series) circuit. (B) OR (parallel) circuit.

Fig. 6-1. AND-OR circuits.

the classes of "female" and "piano player" are quite large, but the class of "female piano player" is just a fraction of the two. The circuit representation of AND is relays in series.

Two relays (M1 and M2) are shown in Fig. 6-1, each having two contacts. To carry power from a source E to a load R1, the relays can be connected in series as shown in Fig. 6-1A. This circuit will pass current, only if *both* relays are closed. This is the same as saying, in logic, that only if *each* statement is true will the two be true. Should one statement be false, one relay will remain open and no current will pass.

If the contacts are connected in parallel as shown in Fig. 6-1B, current from E will flow if either M1 or M2 is closed, or if both are closed.

The two states of true and false can be symbolized by any two opposite conditions. Some of these are:

True	False
Closed	Open
Pulse	No pulse
Positive	Negative

In computer logic, true is designated as 1, or a closed circuit; and false is 0, or an open circuit. From the circuits of Fig. 6-1,

53

it is not difficult to visualize the various conditions shown in Tables 6-1 and 6-2.

For a series circuit, M1 can have a value of either 1 or 0 (closed or open), and so can M2. Thus, there are four possible combina-

Table 6-1. AND circuit truth table.

M1	M2	Circuit
1	1	1
0	1	0
1	0	0
0	0	0

tions, as shown in Table 6-1. But only when M1 = 1 *and* M2 = 1 will the circuit be complete, and only then will current flow through the load.

For a parallel circuit, there are the same four possible combinations. But, if *either* M1 = 1 *or* M2 = 1, or if M1 = 1 *and* M2 = 1, the circuit will be closed.

Table 6-2. OR circuit truth table.

M1	M2	Circuit
1	1	1
0	1	1
1	0	1
0	0	0

Negation, or the denial of a statement, is vital to logic ("No A is B; some A is not B"). In computer logic, if one position of a two-position switch is A, the other position is not-A, written as an A with a bar over it ($\overline{A}$). (In some logical systems this is

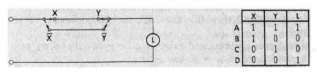

	X	Y	L
A	1	1	1
B	1	0	0
C	0	1	0
D	0	0	1

(A) Circuit.   (B) Truth table.

Fig. 6-2. A logical problem.

shown as A^1.) An example of negation is shown in Fig. 6-2A. Here, a light L is controlled by two wall switches X and Y. Again there are only the four possibilities shown in Fig. 6-2B.

54

Since there is an output (light) for A and D, but none for B and C, it is possible to write for A:

$$L = X \cdot Y \quad \text{Light on} = X \text{ and } Y$$

And for D:

$$L = \overline{X} \cdot \overline{Y} \quad \text{Light on} = \text{not-X and not-Y}$$

A parallel connection is impossible; both switches must be in series for the light to go on. Hence, if A is true and D is true, the combination of both can be only an OR circuit.

Moreover:

$$L = \overline{X} \cdot \overline{Y} + X \cdot Y$$

In other words, since switches X and Y each have only two positions and both must be the same, there are only two possible paths for L to be connected; $\overline{X} \cdot \overline{Y}$ is one, and the other is $X \cdot Y$. These rules of logic are summarized in Fig. 6-3.

LOGICAL FUNCTIONS

All of these theories are the bases for routing data through a computer. One example will serve to show how logical circuits work. Suppose two digits—the Y could be 00, 01, 10, or 11—are to be added. It is obvious that there will be a sum of 1 only if the digits are different, such as 0 and 1 or 1 and 0. If the digits are 0 and 0, their sum will of course be 0; and if they are both 1, there will be a 0 sum (but with a carry of 1). Thus an adder can be made, using a set of logical circuits.

Fig. 6-4 shows two circuits. The one in Fig. 6-4A can be written as:

$$XY(X + Z) (Y + XZ + W) T$$

In other words, the current *must* go through XY; it has no choice. But it may go through either X or Z in the parallel circuit, or through both X and Z. It may then go through either Y, Z and X together; or W; through any two; or through all three. Finally, the current *must* go through T.

Since the Y at the left of the circuit is in series, it may appear anywhere in the line. So the formula can be rewritten as:

$$X(X + Z) Y(Y + XZ + W)T$$

In the foregoing formula, when X and Z in parallel are both closed, the same current will flow through them that flows through X in series. Or the current through X will be the same as the current through it and through X and Z in series. So:

$$X(X + Z) = X$$

55

Symbol	Logic	Relay or Contact	Meaning	Circuit
1	True	Closed	The statement is true, the circuit is closed.	
0	False	Open	The statement is false, the circuit is open.	
·	Series	A and B	A is in series with B.	A B
+	Parallel	A or B	A is in parallel with B.	A B
$\overline{A}$	Not A		Opposite of A (If A = 0, $\overline{A}$ = 1; if A = 1, $\overline{A}$ = 0).	

(A) Basic rules.

Logic	Meaning	Circuit
0·0 = 0	An open in series with an open is open.	
0·1 = 0	On open in series with a closed is open.	
1·1 = 1	A closed in series with a closed is closed.	
$A \cdot \overline{A} = 0$	A switch in series with its negation is open.	A $\overline{A}$

(B) Series circuits.

Logic	Meaning	Circuit
0 + 0 = 0	An open in parallel with an open is open.	
0 + 1 = 1	An open in parallel with a closed is closed.	
1 + 1 = 1	A closed in parallel with a closed is closed.	
$A + \overline{A} = 1$	A switch in parallel with its negation is closed.	A $\overline{A}$

(C) Parallel circuits.

Fig. 6-3. Summary of the rules of logic.

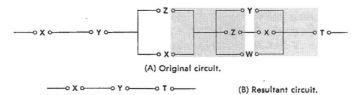

(A) Original circuit.

——o X o——o Y o——o T o—— (B) Resultant circuit.

Fig. 6-4. Circuit reduction.

The same reasoning, applied to $Y(Y + XZ + W)$ gives the formula:

$$Y(Y + XZ + W) = Y$$

By substitution:

$$(XX)(YY)T$$

In logic, A times A equals A (the class of cats that are cats are cats—not cats squared as in algebra). So the formula becomes XYT, as shown by the series circuit in Fig. 6-4B.

The two can thus be considered equivalent circuits in Fig. 6-4. It is clear that X, Y, or T individually can break, or open, the circuit, but that *all three* must be closed in order to complete the circuit. It is also implied that neither Z nor W has any effect whatsoever on the circuit, for neither one is in Fig. 6-4B.

The statement that X, Y, and T must all be closed to complete the circuit, and that any one can open the circuit, is true for all single-series contacts. Notice that Z and W are in parallel with the other switches. For example in the Z + X portion of the circuit, X alone is also in series in another part of the circuit. Hence it must be closed for the circuit to be complete. And if X is closed ($X = 1$), Z just does not count: whether Z is closed or open, current will flow through $X = 1$ in parallel. (Z does affect the circuit if X is open; but since there is an incomplete circuit, this effect can be disregarded.

Thus the two circuits have the same action, but the one in Fig. 6-4B is much simpler.

A block diagram of a circuit can be rearranged in a number of ways through the use of logical relationships. These rearrangements may not be too obvious from the original, but the simpler and more direct arrangement will serve the same function. Refer to Fig. 6-5 as we prove that $A + \overline{A}B$ is the same as $A + B$:

$$A + \overline{A}B = A(B + \overline{B}) + \overline{A}B \text{ (since } B + \overline{B} = 1)$$
$$= AB + A\overline{B} + \overline{A}B$$
$$= A(B + \overline{B}) + B(A + \overline{A})$$
$$= A + B$$

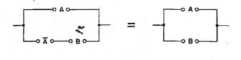

A	Ā	B	CIRCUIT
1	0	1	1
1	0	0	1
0	1	1	1
0	1	0	0

A	B	CIRCUIT
1	1	1
1	0	1
0	1	1
0	0	0

Fig. 6-5. Circuit equivalents.

By substituting values of 1 for A and B, and 0 for $\overline{A}$ and $\overline{B}$ (since, by definition, $A = 1$, $B = 1$, $\overline{A} = 0$, and $\overline{B} = 0$), it is possible to also prove mathematically that these equations are all equal.

LOGICAL CIRCUITS

So far we have been showing strictly logical relationships. In order to use these relationships in computers, the specialized

+   OR   OR GATE, BUFFER

·   AND   AND GATE   Fig. 6-6. Circuit symbols.

$\overline{A}$ NOT   INVERTER

language in Fig. 6-6 was developed. These logical symbols must not be confused with arithmetic operations. For example, the plus sign (+) does not mean "add"—it is logical OR, and its circuit is called an OR gate or buffer. A dot, parentheses ( ), or absence of a sign all signify logical AND, called the AND gate. The symbol I stands for an inverter, which changes A to not-A, the symbol of which is $\overline{A}$.

Using logical symbols it is possible to draw all types of computer functions. Fig. 6-7 shows four possible outputs for logical AND. They are $X \cdot Y$, $X \cdot \overline{Y}$, $\overline{X} \cdot Y$, and $\overline{X} \cdot \overline{Y}$.

X   Y $X \cdot Y$ X   Y $X \cdot \overline{Y}$

X   Y $\overline{X} \cdot Y$ X   Y $\overline{X \cdot Y}$

Fig. 6-7. Basic AND-circuit functions.

$X \cdot Y$ will have an output only if X and Y are both present; $X \cdot \overline{Y}$ will have an output only if X and not-Y are applied to the gate; $\overline{X} \cdot Y$ will permit an output only for not-X and Y; and not-X and not-Y are both required for an output in the last example. Likewise, Fig. 6-8 gives four possibilities for logical OR.

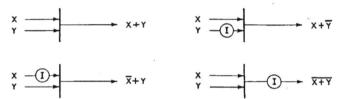

Fig. 6-8. Basic OR-circuit functions.

Suppose a given computer function requires $(A + B)$ $(A + C)$ $(B + \overline{C})$ from inputs A, B, and C. Three OR circuits are used; the first produces $A + B$, the second $A + C$, and the third (along with the inverter), $B + \overline{C}$. All three then go into the AND circuit to provide the proper output, as shown in Fig. 6-9.

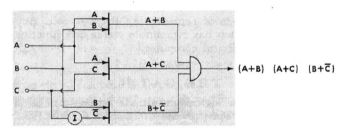

Fig. 6-9. Development of a logical statement.

CHAPTER 7

Basic
Logical Circuits

This chapter will show how the logical circuit blocks discussed in Chapter 6 can be made to operate. Being exact opposites, the binary numbers 1 and 0 used in logical circuits can be represented by several actions and counteractions. Several possibilities are:

0	1
Zero voltage	Positive voltage
No current	Current
Negative pulse	Positive pulse
Low voltage	High voltage
Zero voltage	Negative voltage
No pulse	Pulse

Here are six methods of representing the *1–0* pair. Actually, almost any cricuit which has two stable states can function as a logical element in a digital computer.

THE GATE

The gate is the basic logical circuit. As its name implies, it is a switch that is either open or closed. There is an AND gate and an OR gate, corresponding to their logical counterparts; and each gate has a number of inputs. However, the AND gate will provide an output only if *all* input signals are present. In the OR gate (buffer), there will be an output if *any* of the input signals are present.

The fundamental gate circuit is a simple switch connecting input to output, as in Fig. 7-1A. When this switch is open, the signals (in this example, pulses) cannot pass from the input to the output. Not until the switch is closed do the signals pass from the input to the output. Although seemingly quite basic, this is the action of all gate circuits, however complex.

Consider the single-diode gate in Fig. 7-1B. A series of pulses again is the input. DC bias (+E_K) is applied through R2 to the cathode, and the output is from the junction of R2 and the cathode. With no input to gate lead (R1), there is no conduction because the cathode is positive with respect to the anode. As a re-

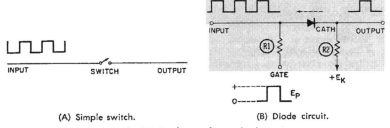

(A) Simple switch. (B) Diode circuit.

Fig. 7-1. Fundamental gate circuits.

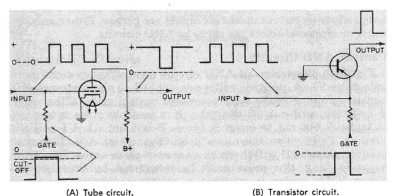

(A) Tube circuit. (B) Transistor circuit.

Fig. 7-2. Tube and transistor gate circuits.

sult, no signal can pass from input to output. In essence, the diode is an open circuit like the switch in Fig. 7-1A. Let us see what happens when a square-wave gate voltage (E_P) is applied to the circuit. Being larger than the DC bias, E_P makes the cathode more negative than the anode, and the diode conducts. For the duration of this gate step, a signal can pass from input to output; but as shown in Fig. 7-1B, the gate voltage allows only one pulse to pass.

Although this circuit is a true gate, it has the disadvantage of reducing the signal passing through the circuit. Gain can be obtained by using active circuit elements such as tubes or transistors. Fig. 7-2A shows a triode amplifier gate. It is normally cut off by a negative bias applied to the gate lead. However, a gate step signal raises the very negative grid voltage to just above cutoff. The tube conducts and thereby amplifies the pulse from the input. As in all tube circuits, the signal is inverted as shown. The voltage drop across the plate-load resistance is the output.

The grounded-base transistor circuit in Fig. 7-2B is also an amplifier gate. The collector is negative, and when the emitter

61

voltage rises to slightly above zero, the transistor conducts. A positive gate voltage to the emitter then allows the gate to pass a signal.

The circuits in Figs. 7-1 and 7-2 are true gates, but they are limited to stop-or-go functions. The logical connectives of AND and OR, which are more useful in computers, are beyond their capacity.

AND CIRCUITS

The AND circuit takes a number of input signals, but does not produce an output unless *all* inputs are proper. Either vacuum tubes or semiconductors can serve as AND circuits.

Pentode AND Circuits

Fig. 7-3A illustrates an AND circuit using a sharp-cutoff pentode tube V1. A positive voltage is applied to the screen, and a negative voltage to the suppressor and control grids. Either grid, if negative, will cut off the tube. If a positive pulse is applied to input A but not to input B (or to B but not A), V1 will not conduct. Only when there is a positive pulse at A and another positive pulse at B will there be an output pulse across R1. Being negative-going, this pulse must be reinverted by inverter amplifier V2 in order to produce a positive pulse (representing binary 1) at output C.

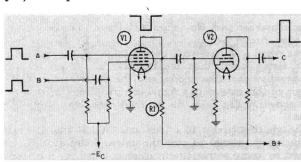

(A) Circuit.

(B) Symbol. (C) Switch circuit.

Fig. 7-3. AND gates.

The AND circuit symbol discussed in Chapter 6 and shown in Fig. 7-3B thus stands for a circuit which requires an input from both A and B in order to provide an output. Another AND, in Fig. 7-3C, is simply two switches in series. A *1* is represented by a closed switch, and a *0* by an open switch. Again, only when A and B are both closed will there be an output current across R.

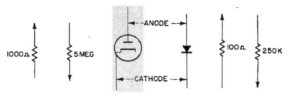

Fig. 7-4. Diode action.

Diode AND Circuits

A diode (Fig. 7-4) can also act as a switch. A vacuum tube will conduct only if its plate is more positive than its cathode. In this forward, or conducting, direction, the resistance of a vacuum tube is about 1000 ohms (in gas-filled diodes it is much less). In the reverse direction, or from plate to cathode, the resistance is very high—about 5 megohms or more. The semiconductor diode is much like its vacuum-tube counterpart. In the forward direction the resistance is 100 ohms or less; but in the reverse, or non-conducting, direction the diode is in effect an open circuit. (This resistance, although measurable, is around 250,000 ohms or more.) Acting as a switch between a low and a high resistance, the diode has many uses—one is in the AND circuit.

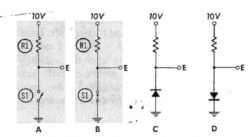

Fig. 7-5. Switching action of a diode.

This switching action can be seen from Fig. 7-5. At A the voltage source is in series with a switch and a load R1 to ground, and E is the output voltage. Two voltage-output states are possible, depending on the action of switch S1. If open as at A, the output voltage will be "high." But if switch S1 is closed as at B, the output voltage will be "low"—in this case, zero or ground.

63

The diode acts like a switch because at C in Fig. 7-5, it is not conducting and hence output voltage E is high; but when its anode is positive, current will flow and the output voltage will be low as in D.

In the diode AND circuit in Fig. 7-6, the anodes go to the +50-volt supply through a common load R1. E_0 is the voltage output, and there are three inputs—E_1, E_2, and E_3—to the diode cathodes. (Since their resistance is very low with respect to R1

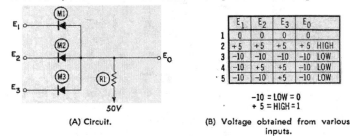

	E_1	E_2	E_3	E_0	
1	0	0	0	0	
2	+5	+5	+5	+5	HIGH
3	−10	−10	−10	−10	LOW
4	−10	+5	+5	−10	LOW
5	−10	−10	+5	−10	LOW

−10 = LOW = 0
+ 5 = HIGH = 1

(A) Circuit.

(B) Voltage obtained from various inputs.

Fig. 7-6. A diode positive AND circuit.

when the diodes are conducting, the drop across them is disregarded in the following examples.) If all cathodes are at zero voltage as in example 1, all three diodes will conduct and the output voltage will be zero. When the inputs are all +5 volts— which is "high" in this example—the output also is "high" as shown at 2. If all inputs are "low," −10 volts here, the output will be "low" as in 3. Now, when one diode input is lower than the others as in 4, the output will still be low. The reason is that M1, with −10 volts on its cathode and +50 volts to its anode (through R1), conducts and lowers the output voltage to −10 volts. The other two diodes cannot conduct because they each have +5 volts at the cathode and −10 volts on the anode. These two are at cutoff (nonconducting) and the output voltage is low because one diode is in effect a short circuit and transfers the −10 volts to the output. In example 5, the inputs to the two diodes are low; so the output voltage remains low because M1 and M2 conduct.

Thus, in this or any AND circuit, *any* low input will keep the output low; the output will be high only if E_1 *and* E_2 *and* E_3 are all high. The −10 volts is "low," or 0; and +5 volts is "high," or 1. Hence, if *all* inputs are 1, the output will be a 1. Otherwise, it will be a 0.

The circuit in Fig. 7-6 is known as a positive AND circuit because its "high" input voltage is more positive than its "low."

Reversing both the diodes and the supply voltage (Fig. 7-7) produces a negative AND circuit. Here −6 volts is "high," or a 1;

64

and zero volts is "low," or a 0. If E_1 is "low," for example, the diode will conduct, placing all cathodes at zero voltage. E_2, which is "high" in this case with -6 volts on its anode, cannot conduct. Thus, the circuit is a negative AND because the "high" input voltage is more *negative* than the "low."

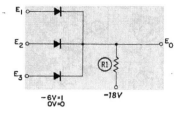

Fig. 7-7. A diode negative AND circuit.

Transistor AND Circuits

Unlike diodes, transistor AND gates will provide gain. Fig. 7-8 shows two transistors with their collector-emitter paths connected in series. The input to the bases controls the output. For this circuit, -6 volts is a 1 and zero volts a 0. (Because of feedback, X2 should turn on before and turn off after X1.)

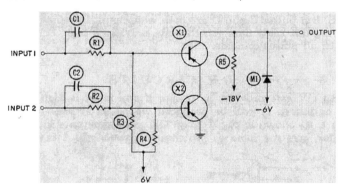

Fig. 7-8. A cascade transistor gate.

A transistor parallel gate is shown in Fig. 7-9. All inputs are to the transistor bases, one to each base. R7 is the common load for all collectors.

AND gate pulses or levels are not always of the same duration to each input; so it is quite possible for the gate to detect a coincidence among several inputs. The AND gate in Fig. 7-10 shows a standard timing pulse B as one input. The other input is a pulse A which, in its travels, has become wider than normal. There will be an output pulse C, only when pulses A and B

65

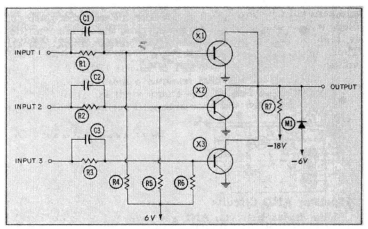

Fig. 7-9. A parallel transistor gate.

coincide and permit the AND gate to provide a 1. Fig. 7-11 shows another example, where four pulses are applied to the gate. The single pulse at A falls at the same time as the center of the three at B. But pulses C and D are both wider and, since they are high during this same time (*t*), the gate provides a high, or 1, output when all pulses coincide.

OR CIRCUITS

An OR gate provides an output if *any* input is high. That is, an output (a 1) will be produced whenever at least one input is a 1. As shown in Fig. 7-12 an OR gate, sometimes known as a buffer, acts the same as switches in parallel. If A is closed *or*

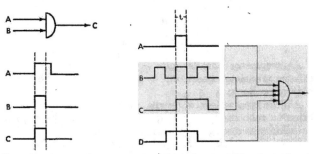

Fig. 7-10. Effect of a timing pulse on an AND gate.

Fig. 7-11. Using an AND gate to detect coincidence.

if B is closed, current flows from E through R as the output. This is a nonexclusive OR, which means simply that if A = 1 or B = 1 *or if both are 1,* there will be an output of 1. In the exclusive OR, there is an output only if A = 1 or B = 1, *but not if both equal 1.*

| (A) Symbol. | (B) Switch circuit. |

Fig. 7-12. The OR buffer.

Diode OR Circuits

The diode logic circuit in Fig. 7-13 performs the OR function in which any single high input will produce a high output. This positive OR circuit is the same as the negative AND in Fig. 7-7; the only difference is in how the circuits are used. All three cathodes in Fig. 7-13 return to −50 volts through a resistance R1. If all anodes return to zero volts as in example 1, or to −5 volts, they will all conduct, since in both instances the cathodes are more negative.

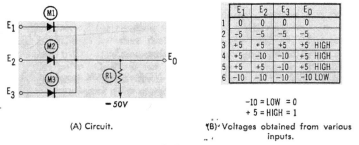

	E_1	E_2	E_3	E_0
1	0	0	0	0
2	-5	-5	-5	-5
3	+5	+5	+5	+5 HIGH
4	+5	-10	-10	+5 HIGH
5	+5	+5	-10	+5 HIGH
6	-10	-10	-10	-10 LOW

−10 = LOW = 0
+ 5 = HIGH = 1

(A) Circuit.   (B) Voltages obtained from various inputs.

Fig. 7-13. A diode positive OR circuit.

In this example −10 volts is low, or 0; and +5 volts is high, or 1. In example 3 all anodes go to +5 volts and the output is high. In 4, however, only anode M1 goes to +5 volts. The +5 volts on its anode causes M1 to conduct. With almost no resistance in its conducting direction, E_0 becomes +5 volts. Thus diodes M2 and M3 have +5 volts on their cathodes but −10 volts on their anodes, and this condition cuts them off. For the OR circuit *any* high

67

input, or a 1, causes a high output. Fig. 7-13 is a positive OR; reversing the diodes and voltage supply provides a negative OR.

NOR CIRCUITS

Any group of diodes can act as either an OR circuit or an AND circuit, depending on the polarity and purpose. Positive AND is the same as a negative OR except that the output is *high* only if *all inputs* are high, while for a negative OR the output is *low* if *any* of the inputs are low.

Conversely, negative AND is the same as a positive OR except that the output is *low* only if *all* inputs are low, while for a positive OR the output is *high* if *any* of the inputs are high.

Because of this similarity the NOR circuit has been developed. It can be either an OR or an AND, depending on conditions. The

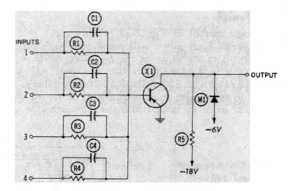

Fig. 7-14. A transistor NOR circuit.

circuit in Fig. 7-14 is a transistor NOR gate. It consists of a clamped saturating common-emitter stage with resistance-coupled parallel-base inputs, and uses base capacitors to provide faster switching times. The circuit performs as an OR gate for both level and pulse inputs with −6 volts as logical 1, or as an AND gate with zero volts as logical 1.

CHAPTER 8

Counters

In a digital computer, numbers represent instructions as well as quantities. Hence, circuits that count are of prime importance.

Industrial electronics finds many uses other than computation for high-speed, direct-reading electronic counters. For example, they can control a manufacturing operation by activating an alarm or stopping the mechanism after a preselected total has been reached.

Any electrical, mechanical, or optical action which can be converted into electrical impulses can be counted and thus controlled. Some conversion devices are photocells, magnetic coils, and switches, as well as transducers for pressure, temperature, velocity, acceleration, and displacement. A number of electronic and electromechanical configurations are possible by using tubes, transistors, and relays in multivibrator, flip-flop, staircase, and blocking-oscillator circuits.

Many electronic-counter circuits are similar to those found in radios, TV's and especially test equipment, because counting and frequency measurement are closely related. Just as it is possible to use a meter for reading the number of pulses per second, it is also possible, now that their frequency is known, to determine the time interval of the pulses by counting the number that pass a given point. Circuits can be designed to operate in either the conventional decade (denary) or the binary numbering system, or both. Readout may consist of direct-reading electrical signals, punched tape, signal lights, alarms, mechanical functions, or any combination of these. Moreover, the information can be obtained without being destroyed, just as a subtotal can be obtained from an ordinary adding machine. This permits continued use of the data.

BINARY COUNTERS

Binary circuits are designed to count in the two-numbered system. The counters are a series of two-state devices such as tubes, transistors, or magnetic cores.

The basic counter is the bistable tube multivibrator, or two-state flip-flop, with a common-cathode load as shown in Fig. 8-1.

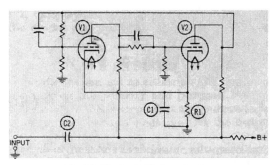

Fig. 8-1. The basic flip-flop circuit.

With no input, one tube conducts more heavily and, because of feedback, is driven into saturation. The heavy current flowing through cathode resistor R1 keeps the other tube cut off. This circuit has two stable states—V1 conducting and V2 off, and V1 off and V2 conducting. It will remain in one state until the arrival

Pulse	V1	V2	Indication
	off	on	0
	on	off	1
2	off	on	0
	on	off	1
	off	on	0
2	on	off	1

Fig. 8-2. Counting with a flip-flop.

of a positive pulse through C2. This pulse will appear at the grids of both tubes, causing the conducting tube to be cut off and the other to start conducting hence, to flip or flop.

In order to count, it is necessary to designate the on-off states. As shown in Fig. 8-2 "V1 off—V2 on" is a 0, and "V1 on—V2 off"

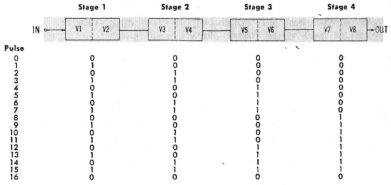

Fig. 8-3. Binary counting with a four-stage flip-flop.

70

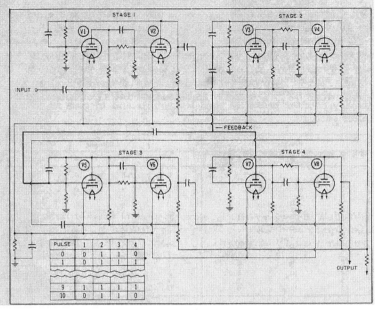

PULSE	1	2	3	4
0	0	1	1	0
1	0	1	1	1
9	1	1	1	1
10	0	1	1	0

Fig. 8-4. A decimal counter circuit.

is a 1. Starting with either a 1 or a 0 as shown, two pulses are thus required to return the circuit to its initial state.

A four-stage flip-flop counter is shown in Fig. 8-3. Since the stages are in series, the first stage counts by 2, the second by 4, the third by 8, and the fourth by 16. This means that after each 16 pulses to the input of the first stage, the entire counter is returned to its all-zero state. For digital computers which operate on the binary system, a count by 16 is useful; but sometimes a count by ten also is needed.

DECADE COUNTERS

A binary-counting circuit can be converted to decimal, or count-by-10, by the use of feedback. Fig. 8-4 is a schematic of a four-stage counter. Without feedback, the eight tubes (in four stages) count by 16. However, feedback from the plate of V7 to the grids of V3 and V5 causes the counter to start at 0110 rather than 0000. So, after nine pulses the count will be 1111. The tenth pulse will cause V8 to go from 1 to 0 (from off to on), decreasing the plate voltage and resulting in a negative output pulse. V7, being of opposite state to V8, has a positive pulse which turns on V3 and

71

V5. Hence, after each 10 pulses there is an output and a return to the 0110 condition, in readiness for the next count of 10.

Neon lamps can be connected to the plates of the counter tubes in order to provide a visual indication for each digit from 0 to 10.

Preset counters have a number set into them before counting starts, and when this number is reached it will trigger an output signal. Any decade counter can thus be thought of as a four-stage binary counter preset to read six counts and to give an output after each 10.

Presets			Stages			
A	B	C	1	2	3	4
0			0	0	0	0
1			1	0	0	0
2			0	1	0	0
3			1	1	0	0
4	0		0	0	1	0
5	1		1	0	1	0
6	2		0	1	1	0
7	3		1	1	1	0
8	4		0	0	0	1
9	5		1	0	0	1
10	6	0	0	1	0	1
11	7	1	1	1	0	1
12	8	2	0	0	1	1
13	9	3	1	0	1	1
14	10	4	0	1	1	1
15	11	5	1	1	1	1
16	12	6	0	0	0	0

Fig. 8-5. Preset counting.

Fig. 8-5 shows the preset counting sequence. The ordinary count without any circuit modification is given at A; this is for a pure binary counter. However, if the counter starts with 0010, as in column B, a full count will be indicated after each 12 input pulses; thus the counter is preset to read out at 12. Again, if preset to 0101 as in C, there will be an output after each six pulses. In other words, a preset binary counter that reads out after each 10 pulses is a decade counter, but any number (up to 16) can be preset in a four-stage counter.

The number desired is placed into the counter by turning dials on the front. The readings are converted into *1*'s and inserted into

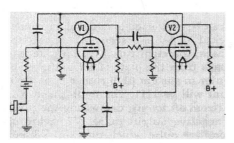

Fig. 8-6. A preset counter circuit.

the proper circuits. For a two-tube flip-flop, a 1 means V1 is on and V2 is off. All stages to be preset to 1 require a positive voltage for the control grid. In a simple circuit like the one in Fig. 8-6, a push button could be used to apply a momentary positive voltage to the grid of V1, causing the tube to conduct and thus be set with a 1. However, electronic circuits are used instead, since push buttons and switches are much too slow. Fig. 8-7 shows how

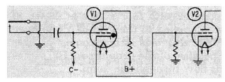

Fig. 8-7. Using a thyratron to preset a counter.

a thyratron tube (V1) is used as an electronic switch. Tube V2 is to be set to a 1 (conducting). After a count has been completed, the output relay closes contacts A. Thyratron V1 fires, placing a positive potential on the grid of V2, which conducts.

Fig. 8-8. A plug-in decade counter.

(Courtesy of Computer Measurements Co.)

Counters are important not only in computer technology, but also in industrial devices for electronic control. One example is the plug-in decade counter in Fig. 8-8, which is used in such equipment as the counter-timer in Fig. 8-9.

RING COUNTERS

Ring counters have their stages parallel-connected in a closed loop. Only one stage is on at any time, and the input pulses are applied to all stages in parallel. For each input pulse, the stage which is on is turned off and the next one turned on.

73

In a four-stage counter (Fig. 8-10A), for instance, only stage 1 is on at the start. The first pulse turns 1 off and 2 on, the second turns 2 off and 3 on, etc., up to the fourth pulse, which turns 4 off and 1 on—the original state of the circuit. Fig. 8-10B shows this switching sequence.

As a frequency divider, a ring counter has only one output for each full series of pulses (N pulses for a counter with N stages), but this output can be taken from *any* stage.

A typical thyratron ring counter with four stages is shown in Fig. 8-11. A negative voltage is applied to the grid of V1 to keep the tube non-conducting. When this bias is overcome, V1 fires and its neon lamp M1 glows because of the drop across R3. Series resistor R6 limits the current flow through the lamp.

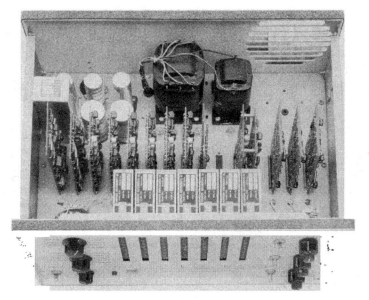

Fig. 8-9. A commercial counter-timer.

In sequence, the counter works this way:
1. Reset push button S1 is closed for a moment. This grounds the grid of V1 and causes the tube to fire. The plate-voltage drop across R3 increases sharply, lighting zero neon M1.
2. Bias voltage applied to all other stages keeps them cut off.
3. The drop across R6, caused by the V1 cathode current, charges C4 as shown. The voltage across R6 is applied to

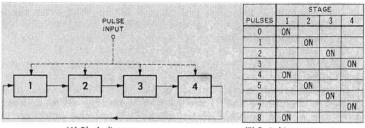

PULSES	STAGE			
	1	2	3	4
0	ON			
1		ON		
2			ON	
3				ON
4	ON			
5		ON		
6			ON	
7				ON
8	ON			

(A) Block diagram.   (B) Switching sequence.

Fig. 8-10. A four-stage ring counter.

the grid of V2 via R8 so that this tube is "primed," or almost ready to conduct.

4. At this point (neon indicator reading zero), a pulse is applied to all grids. This pulse has no effect on V1 because it is already conducting, nor on V3 or V4 because of this bias; but it does cause V2 to conduct. As V2 draws current there is a voltage drop across R12. This voltage, in series with the charge on C4, is applied to the cathode of V1 and, together with the bias on the grid, is enough to cut off V1.

5. Now only V2 is on, with its neon lamp glowing to indicate

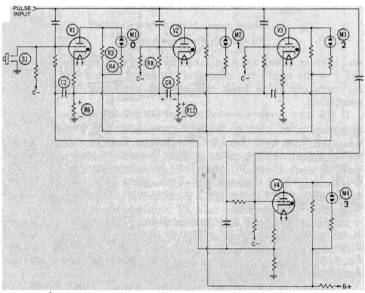

Fig. 8-11. A thyratron ring-counter circuit.

75

a count of 1. The next pulse turns V3 on, and after three pulses V4 is the only tube on.

6. The fourth pulse returns the counter to its original state.

Because ring counters count by 1's, they require more tubes for a given count.

Magnetic cores can also be used as counters. These devices (discussed in Chapters 3 and 7) are inherently binary—they can have only one of two possible states, depending on the direction of magnetization. Fig. 8-12A shows the first two stages of a magnetic core counter. Assume the first core is set (has a 1) and the sec-

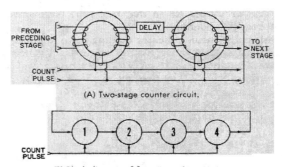

(A) Two-stage counter circuit.

(B) Block diagram of four-stage ring counter.

Fig. 8-12. Magnetic-core counters.

ond is reset (has a 0). A count pulse turns *all* cores to 0 and sends the 1 to the next core, changing the count from 1 0 to 0 1. A delay network holds back the transfer until the count pulse is completed.

If the two cores were connected so that the output from the second was fed back to the first core, the count would be 1 0 to 0 1, and then back to 1 0. This means that two count pulses would return the two-stage unit to its original state, just like in a flip-flop. A string of cores may be interconnected, as in Fig. 8-12B, to make a ring counter. Each count pulse will then move a 1 from one core to the next, starting with 1000, then 0100, 0010, 0001, and back to 1000.

Ring counters have many applications. The decoder in Fig. 8-13 is one example. Here an output is desired for a single code of three numbers. Two main circuit blocks are used: the counter, for determining the number of code pulses received; and the digit register, for code recognition.

Assume the code is 235. The input signal, which consists of groups of pulses, is amplified and sent to the counter. After a

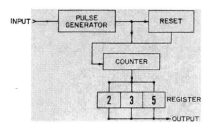

Fig. 8-13. Block diagram of a ring-counter decoder.

group of two pulses has been received, the count of 2 is transferred to the first stage of the digit register and the ring counter is reset. It now receives the 3 and transfers this number to the second stage of the digit register. The same procedure occurs with the 5. After the code 235 has been received and recognized by the digit register, there is an output.

Another use for a ring counter is as a high-speed switch, where computer inputs from several channels—such as A, B, C, and D in Fig. 8-14—are required on a shared-time basis. Each of the four input signals is momentarily applied through rotating switch

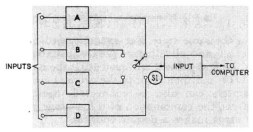

Fig. 8-14. Ring counter as a high-speed switch.

S1, as shown. Fig. 8-15 shows a typical application of the ring counter. Three counter stages (V1, V2, and V3) and two control tubes, or gates, are used. Each gate has a bias voltage on its control grid and a signal on grid 3. Grid 2 is the screen grid of each tube, and R19 is a common plate load for both gates.

When an input pulse is received, V2 is turned on by the drop across the V1 cathode resistor. V4 also conducts, and its signal appears across common plate load R19; but V3 does not conduct because it is biased below cutoff. When the drop across R8 does cause V3 to fire, V5 also conducts, allowing only signal B to appear across R19. In this manner a ring counter can act as a switch and permit only one signal at a time to be sent. The switching rate depends on the source of the pulse applied to the counter tubes.

77

The ring counters described in this chapter all use gas-filled tubes or magnetic cores, but it is also possible to use vacuum tubes.

Flip-flops can be arranged as ring counters by having all but

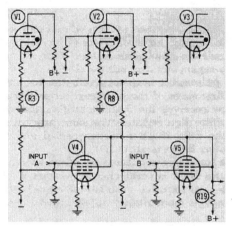

Fig. 8-15. Schematic of a ring-counter switcher.

one stage in the same state. For example, with no input, stage 1 might have a 0 and all others a 1. The counter will then read 0111. After the first pulse it will read 1011; the next pulses change it to 1101, 1110, and then back to the original condition of 0111.

Ring counters can also be connected together with binary counters. Thus, the combination of a five-stage ring counter and one binary stage makes a decade counter.

CHAPTER 9

Calculating
Circuits

In a digital computer the end result comes about through a series of individual operations such as addition or subtraction. These occur in the arithmetic unit—which can be considered the heart of the computer.

The arithmetic unit is made up of numerous two-state stages which operate on the numbers in order to add, subtract, multiply, divide, and compare. For this reason they are called calculating circuits, to differentiate them from the circuits which do logical operations such as AND, OR, or NOT.

NUMBER REPRESENTATION

Binary numbers can be routed through a computer in either serial or parallel fashion (Fig. 9-1). For example, 101101 can

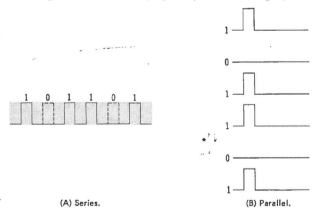

(A) Series.   (B) Parallel.

Fig .9-1. Number representation.

have one signal path, over which the pulses follow one another in series as in Fig. 9-1A; or they can have six signal paths, one for each 1 or 0 as in Fig. 9-1B. Here a pulse is a 1, and no pulse is a 0. Parallel is faster than series since all digits are operated on at once, but requires more elaborate equipment.

Pulses represent binary digits, called *bits*. A computer "word" is made up of several groups, each consisting of a series of bits as shown in Fig. 9-2. Each group, except the first and fifth in this example, can have a maximum of three pulses. (Dotted lines

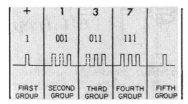

Fig. 9-2. A computer word.

show the absence of pulses for the 0's.) This computer word, decimal number 137, is more than just the number. Sign information is included in the first group. Here a pulse, or 1, is a *plus* meaning a positive number. Conversely, a 0 is a *minus* meaning a negative number. The last group provides a checking pulse, called a *parity bit*. If there is an odd number of pulses in the first four groups, the last group will have a 1 to make an even number; if there is an even number, the last position will have a 0. In this way the total of all pulses is always even—a feature which provides a quick check for errors. As the numbers pass through the computer circuits, the total number of pulses is checked to see if it is odd or even. Any odd number means an error at some point. Incidentally, 137 is presented here in binary-coded octal, where 001 is 1, 011 is 3, and 111 is 7.

Numbers—a series of digits—form computer words which the logical circuits feed to the calculating sections, where several operations are performed. The first one we will look at is addition.

ADDITION AND SUBTRACTION

Just as numbers can be represented in either series or parallel fashion, so can addition. Fig. 9-3 shows a serial adder. The two digits are held separately in registers A and B until fed, one at a time, to the adder circuit. Storage is used for the carry—as in $1 + 1 = 10$, which is 0 carry 1. The sum remains in the C register until further orders.

A parallel representation appears in Fig. 9-4. Again there are two input registers, A and B, as well as storage C for the sum. But there are six adders instead of one, with carry from one to the next, an adder being required for each digit since all are added at once. Note the increase in equipment required for the faster parallel operation.

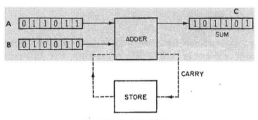

Fig. 9-3. Serial addition.

Computer instructions for addition or subtraction are quite direct. Assume that two numbers, A and B, are available, each in its own register, and that the sum or difference is to be placed in register C for storage until further use.

To add A to B, the computer:
1. Determines if A and B have the same or different signs.
2. If the signs are the same, it adds A to B (using an adder like those in Figs. 9-3 and 9-4), and affixes the common sign. Example: +3 added to +6 is +9; −3 added to −4 is −7. The resultant sum is then sent to register C.

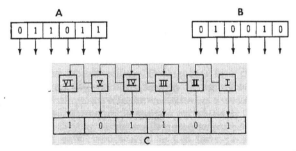

Fig. 9-4. Parallel addition.

3. If the signs differ, it subtracts the negative quantity from the positive one. To subtract in the decimal system, we change the sign of one digit and add. For example, to subtract +4 from +9, +4 is changed to −4 and added to +9, giving +5. In binary, however, the number to be subtracted is converted into its complement, as explained in Chapter 5, and then added.

Hence, before addition can be performed, there is first the problem of recognizing signs. If they are the same, the numbers are directly added; if not, intermediate steps will be required.

81

Sign Comparison

Flip-flops can store other two-state information besides binary numbers. For example, since the sign of a number is either plus or minus, one output of the flip-flop can represent a "plus" and the other a "minus," just as easily as a 1 or 0.

Two flip-flops (F1 and F2), each indicating the sign of a different number, can produce four possible combinations—two for *like* and two for *unlike,* as shown in Fig. 9-5. Four AND gates are used. If the two flip-flops have the same output, one of the AND gates (A1 for a positive sign or A2 for a negative) will

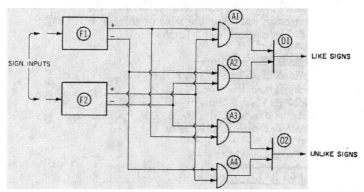

Fig. 9-5. A sign comparison circuit.

have an output; and OR gate O1 will provide an output signal. That is, there will be an output indicating *like* signs, whether both flip-flops have a positive or negative output. One of the two AND gates will provide an output signal; and since an OR gate requires only one input to produce an output, O1 will provide a *like* sign output.

If the two signs are opposites—one positive and one negative—there are only two possible combinations, of course. For either combination, one of the two lower AND circuits will provide an output into the lower OR (O2), indicating an *unlike* sign output and the need for a complement-and-add operation.

In summary, the simple block diagram in Fig. 9-5 is a sign comparator with one of two possible outputs. If the input signals are of the same sign, there will be a *like*-sign output signal; if not, there will be an *unlike*-sign output signal.

Half Adders

After the signs have been compared, the second step is actual addition. For two digits a half adder is used, and there can be a

82

sum ($1 + 0 = 1$, $0 + 1 = 1$) or a carry ($1 + 1 = 10$, which is a 0 sum and a carry 1). The two digits to be added have only four possibilities, as shown in Fig. 9-6A. The digit to be added (A) is the addend and the other (B) is the augend.

Fig. 9-6B shows the half-adder circuit. If both A and B equal 0, there will be no output from the OR gate. Likewise, there will be no output from AND gate A2; hence, no carry. The inverter will have an output, however, because, it changes the carry output from 0 to 1. With a 0 from the OR gate and a 1 from the inverter, there can be no output from A1. Therefore, we have 0 sum and 0 carry. However, if either A or B equals 1, there will be an output from the OR gate to A1, but no output from A2. Now, a 1

ADDEND	AUGEND	SUM	CARRY
0	0	0	0
0	1	1	0
1	0	1	0
1	1	0	1

(A) Possible combinations.

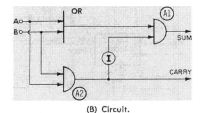

(B) Circuit.

Fig. 9-6. A half-adder diagram.

from the OR gate and a 1 from the inverter are applied to AND gate A1, resulting in a sum output of 1 and no carry output (a 0). If A and B both equal 1, they will pass through the OR gate to produce a 1, and also through AND gate A2 to produce a carry (a 1). The inverter inverts the 1, so a 1 and a 0 are now applied to A1 and there is no sum output—hence, a 0 sum. Therefore, in this example we have a 0 sum and a 1 carry.

It is important to remember that, to produce A plus B, or the sum of the two, this circuit uses an OR gate ($A + B$) as well as AND gates ($A \cdot B$). This is an example of how logical circuits are called on to provide arithmetic operations.

Full Adders

Two half adders form a full adder, as shown in Fig. 9-7. This circuit first produces a partial sum and then adds the carry, which is shifted one place to produce the final sum. In Fig. 9-7A, the addition of 1 and 1 produces a sum of 0, and the carry of 1 is added to the digits in the next place.

Serial addition (Fig. 9-7B) involves taking one pair of digits at a time from the addend and augend, so that only one full adder will be required. Any carry is stored in the delay element for one pulse time. When the carry pulse reaches the delay output, the adder unit will receive the next pair of pulses; and their sum plus the delayed carry produce the sum output from the adder.

Parallel addition (Fig. 9-7C) is faster, of course, since all digits in the addend and augend are added simultaneously. The first half adder produces a sum and a carry. The sum is added to the carry-in by the second half adder to produce the sum output. The carries from the two half adders then go to the AND block for carry-out to the next stage.

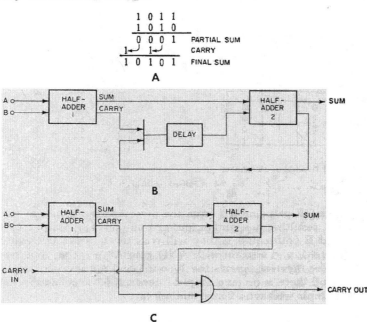

Fig. 9-7. The full adder.

Where only two digits are to be added, the task is simple for the half adder in Fig. 9-6. When both inputs are 0, the output is a 0; if both inputs are 1, the output will still be a 0 with a carry of 1. A 1 in either input means a 1 at the output also.

To add two three-digit numbers, however, there are eight possibilities instead of only four. Fig. 9-8A represents all eight. Aside from all zeroes, there are three different cases, depending on the number of 1's—either one, two, or three. A letter is a 1; and not -A, not -B, etc., is a 0. A is the addend, B the augend, C the carry-in from the last addition, D the sum, and E the carry-out to the next addition.

84

For a single 1, there are three possibilities: $A + \overline{B} + \overline{C}$ $(1 + 0 + 0)$, $\overline{A} + B + \overline{C}$ $(0 + 1 + 0)$, and $\overline{A} + \overline{B} + C$ $(0 + 0 + 1)$. Hence there is always a *sum*, but never a carry.

For any two *1*'s: $A + B + \overline{C}$ $(1 + 1 + 0)$, $A + \overline{B} + C$ $(1 + 0 + 1)$, and $\overline{A} + B + C$ $(0 + 1 + 1)$ there is a *carry*, but never a sum.

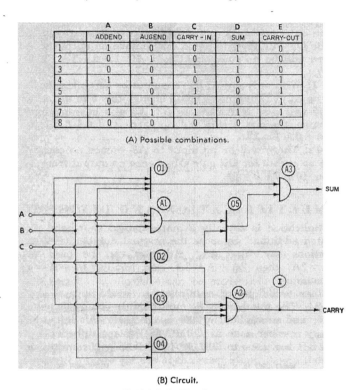

	A	B	C	D	E
	ADDEND	AUGEND	CARRY – IN	SUM	CARRY-OUT
1	1	0	0	1	0
2	0	1	0	1	0
3	0	0	1	1	0
4	1	1	0	0	1
5	1	0	1	0	1
6	0	1	1	0	1
7	1	1	1	1	1
8	0	0	0	0	0

(A) Possible combinations.

(B) Circuit.

Fig. 9-8. Full-adder diagram.

Where every digit is a 1: $A + B + C$ $(1 + 1 + 1)$, there are *both* a carry and a sum. Where every digit is a zero as $\overline{A} + \overline{B} + \overline{C}$ $(0 + 0 + 0)$, there is obviously neither a sum nor a carry.

To follow addition of three-digit numbers, refer to Fig. 9-8B and trace the inputs through the circuit while reading the following explanation. (The I block is the inverter, which changes a 1 to a 0 and a 0 to a 1.)

All 1's: The three OR gates (O1, O2, and O3) each have two 1's. So there is a 1 from each, resulting in three *1*'s in AND gate

85

A2. This provides a carry, which is inverted and appears as a 0 at O5. But the three 1's into A1 provide a 1 input to O5; hence, O5 has an output. O1 has three 1's; so there are two 1's into A3. This produces both a sum and a carry output $(1 + 1 + 1 = 11)$.

Two 1's: The three OR gates (O2, O3, and O4) will each have at least one 1. A2 will have three 1's—hence there will be a carry. AND gate A1 will have two 1's and hence no output. A2 will have an output (carry), but it will be inverted through I. Since OR gate O5 will have no input, it will have no output to A3 and so there will be no sum $(1 + 1 + 0 = 10; 1 + 0 + 1 = 10; 0 + 1 + 1 = 10)$.

One 1: With only one 1, there cannot be three inputs to A2—hence no carry. The inverter will change this 0 to a 1 which OR gate O5 will pass to AND gate A3. A3 also has an input from O1—hence, there is a sum but no carry $(1 + 0 + 0 = 1; 0 + 1 + 0 = 1; 0 + 0 + 1 = 1)$.

All 0's: There will be no input to A2—hence no carry. There will be no output for OR gate O1—hence no output from A3, and no sum $(0 + 0 + 0 = 0)$.

MULTIPLICATION AND DIVISION

Multiplication is actually a mathematical shorthand meaning "repeated addition." Suppose the original number is A, and the instructions say "find 4A." Addition can be used to give $A + A = 2A$, then $2A + A = 3A$, and finally, $3A + A = 4A$, or the answer.

Another technique of multiplication is shifting, as shown in Fig. 9-9A. The number *352* is multiplied by 10 by one shift left, to 3520; and multiplied by 100 by another shift left, to 35,200. A binary number such as 110110 (54) is multiplied by 2 when shifted left one place to 1101100 (108), and again multiplied by 2

```
   SHIFT LEFT IS × 10          SHIFT LEFT IS × 2
        3 5 2 . 0 0                 1 1 0 1 1 0
      3 5 2 0 . 0 0               1 1 0 1 1 0 0
    3 5 2 0 0 . 0 0             1 1 0 1 1 0 0 0
   SHIFT RIGHT IS ÷ 10          SHIFT RIGHT IS ÷ 2
        3 5 2 . 0 0                 1 1 0 1 1 0
          3 5 . 2 0                 1 1 0 1 1
           3 . 5 2                    1 1 0 1
```

(A) Decimal.   (B) Binary.

Fig. 9-9. Multiplication and division by shifting.

when shifted left another place to 11011000 (216) as shown in Fig. 9-9B. Note that for each shift left—multiply by two in binary—each "empty" space receives a 0.

Division, the opposite of multiplication, requires a shift right. For example, starting with decimal 352, a shift right divides by

10 to give 35.2, and a second shift right produces 3.52, which is division by 100. The same applies to binary, where successive shifts right of 110110 produce 11011 and 1101, or a divide by two each time. (See Fig. 9-9B.)

This shifting is done in the shift register. As shown in Fig. 9-10, it consists of several flip-flops connected together so that each one transfers its information to the next flip-flop when the advance input is pulsed.

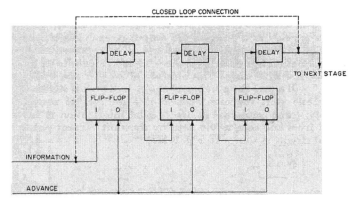

Fig. 9-10. A shift-register diagram.

You'll recall that flip-flops can be made from vacuum tubes, transistors, or any other active devices, and that each flip-flop has two stable states called *set* (1) and *reset* (0). A flip-flop can be said to provide a type of memory. It will remain in its last state until a pulse signifying the opposite state causes it to change. For example, as long as the flip-flop is in the set state, it will remain so until a pulse arrives at the reset input. It will then go to the reset state and remain there until a pulse arrives at the set input. This stability is the reason why the shift register using flip-flops is one of the simplest and most frequently-used digital devices, not only for shifting in multiplication and division, but also for temporary storage of digital data, conversion of this data from serial to parallel or parallel to serial, and generation of pulse patterns. Now we will analyze the basic shift-register operation and give several techniques for generating pulse patterns.

Again refer to Fig. 9-10. The advance line is connected to the zero input of all flip-flops in the shift register. In this circuit, when the line is pulsed the flip-flops in the set (1) state switch to 0, and those in the reset (0) state remain in the 0 state. The output signal from a switching flip-flop is shaped and delayed in the delay interstage circuits, and then directed to the *1* input of the next flip-flop to complete the shift operation. Information can be inserted into the first flip-flop between each shift. The advance pulses will then shift this information through the register until it emerges at the other end.

If the output of a later stage is connected to the input of the first one, the information will travel around the closed loop and return to the first stage. This arrangement, shown by the dotted lines, is known as a cycle distributor. A closed-loop shift register can be used to generate a repetitive pulse pattern. The pattern is preset into the shift register. As the register advances, the preset pattern appears as a pulse at the output of each stage in succession. The pulse pattern will continue to be repeated each time the information travels around the loop and returns to its original location, the first stage. The number of bits in one cycle, or a "word," will equal the number of stages in the shift register.

Magnetic shift registers consist of a number of square-loop magnetic cores connected so that digital information is logically shifted from one core to the next by the shift-current pulse. The general circuit is shown in Fig. 9-11.

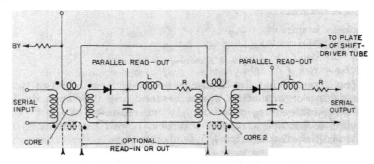

Fig. 9-11. A magnetic-core shift register.

Information is stored in a magnetic core by associating the numbers 0 and 1 with the two residual magnetic states inherent in the cores. With the application of a shift pulse, all cores are switched to the 0 state. If a pulse is now applied to the input winding of core 1, this core will change to the 1 state and remain in this state until another shift pulse is applied. Core 1 will then return to the 0 state, producing a large flux change which results in a voltage at the output winding of the core. This voltage causes current to flow through the diode, charging capacitor C.

After the shift pulse is completed, the capacitor discharges through the pulse-forming inductance and resistance. Current flows in the input winding of core 2, switching it to the 1 state.

In this manner, *1* signals can be transferred down long lines of cores with no effective attenuation. The 0 signal may be transferred from one core to another, since there is no large flux change in the output winding; hence the next core receives no input signal. The ratio of the *1* signal to the 0 signal is an important measure of the electrical efficiency of the register, and for this reason should be as large as possible.

COMPARISON CIRCUITS

The half adder (Fig. 9-6) has an important characteristic which permits its use as a comparison circuit for detecting errors. If two unlike digits are fed into the half adder, it will provide a sum output; but if the digits are alike (0,0 or 1,1), there will be *no* sum output. In other words, the half adder is a detector of equality or inequality.

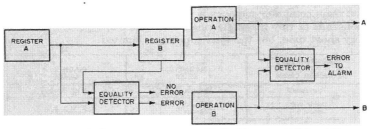

(A) Checking transfer between registers.   (B) Checking two parallel operations.

Fig. 9-12. Comparison circuits.

Fig. 9-12 shows two such examples. The number in register A (Fig. 9-12A) is transferred to register B, and the problem is to make sure both registers contain the same number. The half adder compares the contents of A and B, digit by digit. As long as it has no output, this means the digit in A is the same as its respective digit in B. The computer can now clear register A, since A has transferred its contents to B without error. However, an "error" signal means a mistake has been made; so register B must be emptied and the number transferred again.

A second use of the equality detector is shown in Fig. 9-12B. There are two parallel stages, A and B, each performing the same arithmetic problem. The equality detector compares the results of each, digit by digit. Only if they are identical—meaning no error in either state—will the computer proceed to the next step.

CHAPTER 10

Information Storage

Computers require several types of information storage, or memory, determined by whether speed of recall or amount stored is more important. For example, a computer has a small, high-speed memory for split-second insertion and extraction of small amounts of data, a slower but larger storage for information not required at once, and a third one for bulk storage.

These three systems can be seen from the chart in Fig. 10-1. The main computer memory is usually a core matrix made up of thousands of tiny magnetic rings. The data can be retrieved in a very short time, but the total capacity is limited.

MAGNETIC TAPE OR PUNCHED CARDS	MAGNETIC DRUM	MAGNETIC CORES
Low Speed	Medium Speed	High Speed
Unlimited Capacity	High Capacity	Low Capacity
Input-Output	Secondary Memory	Primary Memory

Fig. 10-1. Comparison of the various methods of storage.

A magnetic drum, which is a cylinder with a series of magnetic tracks, forms the back-up, or secondary, memory. Its access time—or how long it takes to find a certain piece of information—is longer than the core system's, but it has a greater storage capacity.

Magnetic tapes and punched cards are the third form of memory. There is no limit to how much information they can store, but their access time is much longer than for other memories.

Other forms also exist. A flip-flop, for example, remembers its last state (either 1 or 0) until triggered into switching its state. However, the three memory devices in Fig. 10-1 are the most important, although others will also be discussed in this chapter.

COMPUTER MEMORY

There is a marked similarity between the computer storage and the human brain. Just as the computer uses simple on-off devices for storage, so it is believed does the human brain receive similar impressions from the nervous system. Neurons, or nerve cells, seem to operate as yes-no devices in sending information to the brain. For example, stored in your brain may be these two bits: "Yes, I will run if I see a bear," and its obverse, "No, I will not run if I do not see a bear." As long as your optic nerve keeps sending the message, "No, I do not see a bear," the brain will respond with, "No, I will not run." But the moment the optic nerve says, "Yes, I see a bear" . . . you know the rest.

Even the most complex paths can be followed, using a series of yes-or-no decisions as in Fig. 10-2A. Through a series of simple switches, one path such as 1-2-3-4 will lead to one action; and by changing any switch, a new path can be charted. In both the brain and the computer, the memory accepts those paths leading to the goal while rejecting all others.

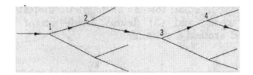

(A) Path as a series of yes-no decisions.

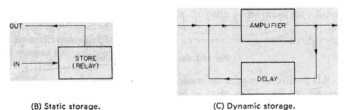

(B) Static storage.   (C) Dynamic storage.

Fig. 10-2. Types of storage.

Storage is either static, as in a latching relay or punched cards where the data remains in one place (Fig. 10-2B); or dynamic, where the data circulates like the pulse in Fig. 10-2C. Here the storage consists of the circulation of the bit through the amplifier. If the amplifier should fail, the pulse would be lost.

Again, the computer and human brain seem to bear a resemblance. The brain apparently stores older memories in a static form (the subconscious), and more recent memories in a dynamic form (the conscious). But the brain has an enormous capacity which no computer memory can even begin to approach. The average brain can store from 10 million to 1 quadrillion (10^8 to 10^{15}) bits! A computer with the same capacity would have to be the size of the Empire State Building. But it would take so long to look up stored data, it would be useless.

Besides being classified according to storage capacity and relative speed as in Fig. 10-1, or whether static or dynamic as in Fig. 10-2, storage systems can also be considered as volatile or nonvolatile. In a nonvolatile, or permanent, memory system the information remains in storage even after the power supply of the computer has been turned off. Examples of this type of storage are magnetic cores, tapes, or drums; paper tape and cards; and photographic film. In volatile memory systems the data disappears when the power is removed. Volatile storage includes delay lines, relays, tubes, transistors, and cathode-ray tubes.

MAGNETIC STORAGE

There are three types of magnetic memory, or storage: (1) cores, consisting of small toroids of magnetic material; (2) tapes, wound onto reels; and (3) drums, made up of short pieces of tape looped around a cylinder.

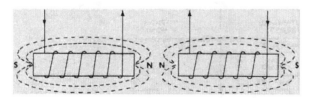

Fig. 10-3. Magnetization of a core.

All forms of magnetic memory depends on the principle, illustrated in Fig. 10-3, that a current through a coil will create a magnetic field in a given direction, and an opposite current will create a magnetic field in the opposite direction. By using a retentive core material, it is possible to store the magnetic field in the core material even after the current flow stops.

Core Memory

One of the most significant advances in memory systems is the magnetic-core memory. The core is a toroid made of a magnetic material such as magnesium manganese or nickel-zinc ferrite, and it can be magnetized in either a clockwise or counterclockwise direction. This means that either a *1* or a *0* can be stored, depending on the direction of magnetic-flux density B, and the core will remain in this state (direction of magnetization).

A hysteresis loop is indicated in Fig. 10-4 for a magnetic core, the flux density B and magnetizing force H are plotted. Let the

92

initial state of the core be $-B_R$. If a pulse of current equal to or greater than $+H_M$ is applied, the flux density will rise to $+B_M$ during the pulse time. When the pulse is removed, the flux will decrease to $+B_R$, or the flux at rest. This condition can be considered the storage of a 1.

If a pulse of opposite polarity equal to or greater than $-H_M$ is then applied, the flux density will move to $-B_M$ and then return to $-B_R$ when the pulse is removed. Thus $-B_R$ can be said to represent the storage of a 0.

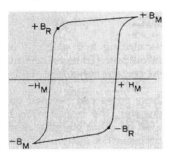

Fig. 10-4. Hysteresis loop.

Again, consider the core starting from $-B_R$, the storage of a 0. If a *negative* pulse is applied, the core will not change its state, but will go to $-B_M$ and then rest again at $-B_R$. Thus, "switching" from one state to another requires a current pulse opposite from the present state of the core.

In the switching process the large rate of change in flux during time t causes an induced voltage.

$$e = -N\frac{d\phi}{dt}$$

where,
N is the number of turns in the output coil,
ϕ is the flux in webers.

This output voltage occurs whenever the core changes its state. From this action a rudimentary memory system can be developed. A pulse of current stores one digit, or bit, of information (either a 1 or a 0) in each core, as shown in Fig. 10-5. When the information is desired, the core in question is pulsed and the output "read." If this information is required in the same location at another time, it is replaced by being regenerated.

Information is placed into this memory system by putting a 1 or 0 in each core. The readout winding also threads the core. When a negative pulse (a pulse in the opposite direction) is applied to the winding, only those cores storing a 1 will be switched

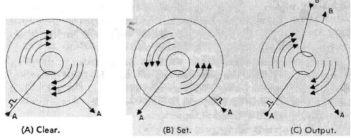

| (A) Clear. | (B) Set. | (C) Output. |

Fig. 10-5. Core magnetization.

and will produce an output; the cores storing a 0 will not be switched and hence will not produce an output. (In some circuits an "inhibit" winding is added to prevent certain cores from being switched.)

Thus, the information retained by these cores can be read out at any time. In this simple system, however, the information is lost when read out unless it is regenerated by other circuits. Also, in the actual computer memory, a switch-matrix system is used to address the cores in order to cut down the number of tubes or transistors needed.

Cores are less than one-sixteenth inch in diameter, which means 10,000 will fit in a 10" × 10" area—or 100 bits per square inch! Cores are mounted on vertical and horizontal wires as shown in Fig. 10-6, and each core can be identified by its intersecting wires

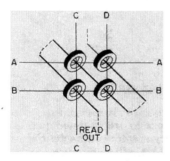

Fig. 10-6. Portion of a memory plane.

such as AC, AD, BC, or BD. Another winding, going through all the cores, is for readout.

A large current flow is required in order to magnetize a core, because the wires go through the core instead of being wrapped around it. The magnetic field created is determined by the amount of current through a coil, multiplied by the number of turns in it, as shown in Fig. 10-7. In this example 250 mils are required,

94

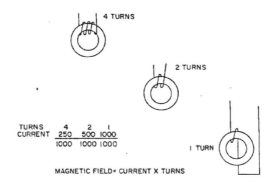

TURNS	4	2	1
CURRENT	250	500	1000
	1000	1000	1000

MAGNETIC FIELD = CURRENT X TURNS

Fig. 10-7. Magnetization of a coil.

with four turns for a product of 1 ampere-turn. With only two turns, 500 mils would be required; and for one turn, a full ampere (1000 mils). Because the "winding" in a core memory is only half of a turn, a large current flows through the wires.

As shown by Fig. 10-7, a current I of a certain size is required to switch a core—anything less will not do so. Fig. 10-8 shows part of a core arrangement or matrix. When V1 fires, a current pulse goes through five cores. But this current is only ½I and is not enough to switch any core. V2 is another tube, also with a plate-current pulse of ½I and going to five cores. So, only the one core at the intersection of these two lines receives the full current I and is switched.

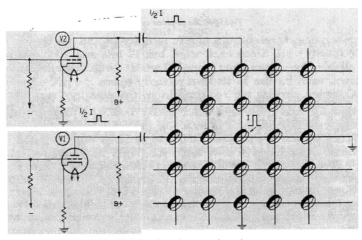

Fig. 10-8. Portion of a core-plane driver.

Since each magnetic core can store only one bit, hundreds of cores are required in a computer memory. Because of their short access time, information can be placed into or read out of them very quickly. Each complete group of cores is a memory plane, as shown in Fig. 10-9. This one has 10 cores on a side, or a total of 100 cores. Since there are 10 planes, there are 1000 cores in all—a small memory in terms of modern computers. A computer word in this example has a total of 10 bits—eight representing the

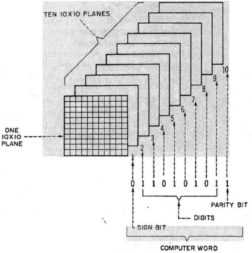

Fig. 10-9. A ten-plane system.

number, one representing a plus or minus sign, and one the checking (parity) bit. Since each word has 10 bits and 1000 bits are available, the memory can store 100 words. In the parallel system shown, each bit lies in its own memory plane.

Complex circuits are required to switch data into and out of a core memory. Since, in this discussion, one driver tube (Fig. 10-8) is needed for each vertical or horizontal line, 1000 tubes would be required for the memory in Fig. 10-9! Actually, a switching matrix is used in order to reduce the number of tubes needed. It is part of the addressing system which locates the desired core.

Magnetic-core systems have several storage functions in a modern computer: a large-capacity main storage system of cores forming the memory; a smaller system which fills up with information and empties at a different rate, commonly known as a buffer store; and a still smaller group for short-term use, known as a register.

96

Two new memory techniques have been developed, although cores are the most widely used. One method involves a plate of ferrite material with tiny holes punched in it; a magnetic field *around* each hole forms the memory bit, and printed wiring is

(Courtesy of Avco Corp.)

Fig. 10-10. A computer tape reader.

used for the read/write connections. In the second technique, extremely thin layers of a magnetic material are deposited on insulators.

Magnetic Tape Storage

Magnetic tapes outside the computer can store vast amounts of information, but their access time is greater than for other memories because the tapes are several hundred feet in length. Fig. 10-10 shows a bank of 15 tapes, each with two spools, serving as the computer input. The IBM 7090 system uses a similar tape storage, as illustrated in Fig. 10-11.

Each tape is wound from one reel onto another, passing at least one magnetic head as shown in Fig. 10-12. The tape usually consists of three layers. Its base is ordinarily a plastic such as *Mylar,* onto which is deposited a very thin layer of iron oxide to form the magnetic substance. A third, protective layer keeps the iron oxide from rubbing off as it moves past the head.

97

The head resembles the core in a magnetic-core memory except for a gap in the magnetic structure. The magnetic flux is contained in the structure and infringes onto the tape across the gap.

As the current passes through the "write" winding, a magnetic field is impressed across the tape. Depending on the direction of the current, a 1 or a 0 will be recorded. If information is recorded on the tape, the same head can be used to reproduce the recorded data. Each recorded section will induce a current flow in the "read" winding as the flux cuts the read coil; and since reading and writing do not occur at the same time, a single winding on a single head can be used for both. In the write function, current flow in the winding will cause a magnetic field for recording. In the read function, a current flow is induced in the head by the passage of a recorded bit. The gap used for both purposes is usually only 0.001 inch or so, and is filled by a small, nonmagnetic shim.

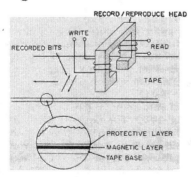

Fig. 10-12. Tape recording.

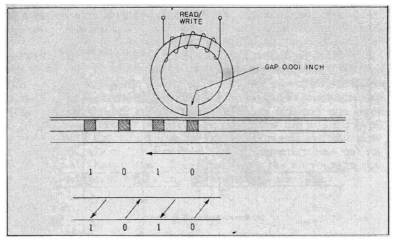

Fig. 10-13. Recording on a magnetic tape.

As shown in Fig. 10-13, a series such as 1010 could be recorded by a single read-write head. In this case a 1 is magnetized in one direction and a 0 in the other.

A single head with write and read amplifiers is shown in Fig. 10-14. Two write amplifiers or drivers are shown, one for each

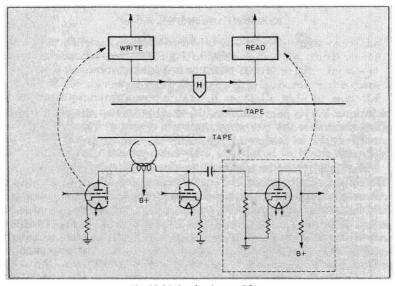

Fig. 10-14. Read-write amplifiers.

99

direction of magnetization. Since read and playback occur at different times, the signal picked up by the same coil winding during the read function is amplified by the read amplifier.

Pulse packing (also discussed in Chapter 3) is a measure of how dense the pulse recording is—in other words, how close together the data are recorded. The higher the pulse density, the less the amount of tape needed for storing information. Fig. 10-15A shows one possible recording method, the return-to-zero (RZ)

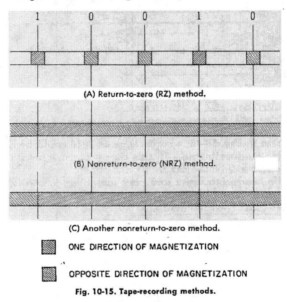

(A) Return-to-zero (RZ) method.

(B) Nonreturn-to-zero (NRZ) method.

(C) Another nonreturn-to-zero method.

ONE DIRECTION OF MAGNETIZATION

OPPOSITE DIRECTION OF MAGNETIZATION

Fig. 10-15. Tape-recording methods.

technique. As its name implies, the magnetization returns to zero after each recorded bit, whether it is a 0 or a 1. The two different directions of magnetic recording for a 1 and a 0 are also depicted.

Pulse density can be increased by use of the nonreturn-to-zero (NRZ) recording system in Figs. 10-15B and C. Fig. 10-15B illustrates one method in which the direction of magnetization changes only in switching from a 0 to a 1 or a 1 to a 0. Where five recorded pulses were required to store 10010 in Fig. 10-15A, in Fig. 10-15B only the changes in digits are recorded. It is also possible to have an NRZ system in which the only time the direction of magnetization changes is to store a 1, as shown in Fig. 10-15C.

Any such increase in pulse density is important, for tapes are required to store huge quantities of data. At a density of 200 bits per inch of tape, a reel of tape 1200 feet long and one-half inch wide can store more than 2,800,000 bits; and lengths of 2400 and 3600 feet are not uncommon. Computer installations often have an entire bank of tape stations which do nothing but store information. One computer with 10 stations, each with a 3600-foot roll, can store more than 85,000,000 individual bits of information. Although this is an enormous amount of data, it is nothing compared with what a human brain can store!

There is a difference between the tape used for audio reproduction, where the sound quality is all-important, and the tape in computers, where the direction of the magnetization—not its amount—is all that matters. For this reason, the currents in the write head are made heavy enough to saturate the tape.

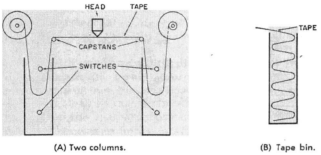

(A) Two columns.　　　　　　　　　(B) Tape bin.

Fig. 10-16. Tape-handling techniques.

Another difference between audio and computer tapes is the matter of starting and stopping. Unlike an audio tape which moves slowly and need not be stopped quickly, computer tape moves at a speed of 100 inches or more per second; and because the computer must pinpoint specific data, it must be able to stop the tape at the proper point with no lost motion.

Data are stored in blocks of computer words occupying around an inch of tape and separated by short sections of blank tape. For example, say the required data are stored in block 856. As the tape moves past the playback head; the counter circuit tied to it would count off the proper block. After stopping at the block, the tape may have to be reversed instantaneously. Because of the many rapid starts and stops, special measures are used to prevent the tape from breaking. A typical system, shown in Fig. 10-16A, is able to start or stop the tape in 0.005 second. Two columns are used, one for each reel. The switches are photoelectric cells that keep the tape loop above the lower switch and below the upper one. Each tape has its own drive motor connected to a servomechanism. When a tape reel starts, it only has to draw

101

from the loop—not from the entire tape. The other reel and its motor move the tape to keep the loop at the proper size. In this way, quick stops and starts are possible without breaking the tape.

In some high-speed applications the tape reels feed into bins, where the tape lies in loose folds as shown in Fig. 10-16B.

One disadvantage of tape is its long access time. In extreme cases where the data are at the end of a 3600-foot tape, the computer would have to search the entire 3600 feet. The magnetic drum discussed next has a much shorter access time.

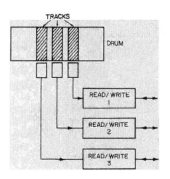

Fig. 10-17. Tracks on a storage drum.

Magnetic-Drum Memory

Magnetic tapes can store enormous quantities of data, but their speed restriction limits their use. By using a magnetic drum, the time needed to locate the needed information is greatly reduced. Fig. 10-17 shows one method using three tracks, each consisting of a strip of magnetic tape with a combination recording-playback head. Data can be made available almost instantly by this system.

A magnetic drum usually rotates at 1200 to 15,000 rpm, 3600 rpm being average. Information can always be located, on a single track, in less than one revolution. In Fig. 10-18, for example, if the head is at point X on the drum, the next desired spot of data could be at Y, almost a full revolution away; or at Z, only one-quarter turn away. The maximum access time for a drum rotating at 3600 rpm is 0.0083 second, or 8.3 milliseconds—the time required for the drum to make one complete revolution. The average time is roughly 4 milliseconds.

With parallel magnetic tracks and at a density of 1000 pulses per square inch, each drum can store millions of bits of data. The number of bits on each track depends on the drum's diameter, which varies from four to fifteen inches; and the number of tracks depends, of course, on the width of the drum.

102

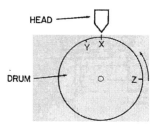

Fig. 10-18. Information is less than one revolution away.

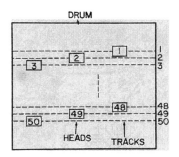

Fig. 10-19. Head placement.

The area beneath a head is a magnetic track made up of tiny bits of recorded data. One hundred recordings per inch are often used, with more than thirty tracks per inch along the width of the drum.

Even with small recording-playback heads it would be impossible to place 200 heads across a 12-inch drum, for this would leave only 0.06 inch for each head. Instead, the heads are staggered as in Fig. 10-19 so that their positions overlap. This allows closer spacing of the magnetic tracks—in this example there are 50. It is not necessary for each head to have a separate read-write amplifier; switching can be used. In Fig. 10-20, two heads (A and B) in a series of perhaps 50 or 100 are shown, and a tube controls the switching for each head. The cathode of V1 has a large negative voltage which cuts off the tube. This negative voltage is coupled directly to head A and is applied to the anodes of the diode pair to keep them cut off. In order for head A to read or play back, a positive voltage is applied to the grid of V1. This tube conducts, and the drop across the cathode resistor makes the cathode voltage positive. This positive voltage permits the diodes to conduct and thereby turn head A on so it can either read or write. In the same manner, the other heads can be activated by switching their respective control tubes.

Switching is used for reading a word from its location or for writing a word in a certain place. Each track consists of a series of computer words separated by short empty spaces, as shown in Fig. 10-21. Control circuits turn on the proper head at the beginning of the word to be read, and turn it off at the end.

For identification, a separate track on the drum carries a series of prerecorded timing pulses which are read by a head. Its output gives the precise location of any spot on the drum as it passes the head. Suppose the instructions from the computer's control section are: "Read word 35 on track 103." The address selector (Fig.

103

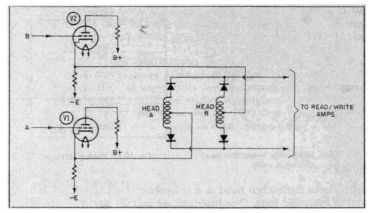

Fig. 10-20. Diode isolation of tape heads.

10-22) is preset to a count of 35, and the pulses from the drum timing track are read into a word counter. The latter, as its name implies, counts the timing pulses that correspond to the words on track 103. When the count of 35 is reached, the comparison circuit produces an output signal, telling the control circuit to switch on the head for track 103. After reading the word, the head goes off when it reaches the spacer immediately following the word.

A typical magnetic drum (Fig. 10-23) is 7.5 inches in diameter and runs at speeds of 1800 to 3600 rpm. With 130 pulses per inch there will be 3072 pulses per track. Hence an 85-track model will contain 261,120 bits, and a 280-track, 860,160 bits. Larger drums, with an 18.5-inch diameter, can store 6,210,500 bits on 825 tracks.

Magnetic discs, which look like phonograph records, can store enormous amounts of data. For example, eight discs on both sides, with 64 tracks per inch and a density of 360 bits per inch, can store more than 250,000,000 bits!

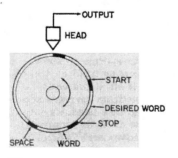

Fig. 10-21. Spacing of computer words on drum.

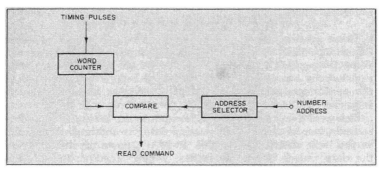

Fig. 10-22. Selection of computer words.

Magnetic drums often receive information directly from the tape storage, so that it will be available the instant it is required.

Magnetic systems are often classified according to type of access. Core memories may be written or read out at any point; hence they are known as random access. A tape requires reading along the entire length or until the required information is found, and for this reason are called serial-access storage forms. A drum requires random location of the track and then a series search for the specific data—hence the name, random serial.

Fig. 10-23. Drum file unit of a data processer.

OTHER STORAGES

There are several other memory, or storage, devices of lesser importance than the magnetic ones. Computers often require a *delay line,* which is a form of storage. In a magnetic-core shift register, for example, a delay is needed before a 1 is shifted to the next stage; and in some forms of addition, a carry delay is required.

Delays of a few microseconds, or up into the hundreds of microseconds, can be obtained by passing data through a medium such as the tank of mercury in Fig. 10-24A. Quartz crystals convert the data pulses into sonic pulses, which "crawl" through the mercury at the speed of sound and hence are delayed. At the other end of the tank, a second transducer reconverts the sonic

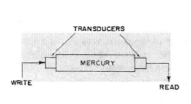

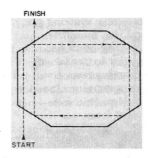

(A) Mercury type.   (B) Prism type.

Fig. 10-24. Delay lines.

pulses into electrical pulses. This delay resembles a thunderstorm, where the lightning flash is seen several seconds before the thunderclap is heard—the reason being the tremendous difference between the speeds of sound and light.

There are various types of delay lines. Mercury tanks are useful for low pulse rates; and in a large tank, it is possible to use several different delay paths without interference.

Quartz-crystal transducers transfer the pulses to and from the tank, and quartz can also be used as a delay with a number of internal reflections. As shown in Fig. 10-24B, the path around the crystal is five times longer than the direct one. Moreover, the delay can be increased even further by using a many-sided polygon instead of the one shown.

Magnetostrictive delay lines have the characteristic of becoming deformed when strained by a magnetic field, and can thus send a wave down a coil of wire to the end. Special transmission

106

lines are also used to delay a radio-frequency signal traveling along it.

Electromechanical relays as a form of storage were used in the very early digital computers. As discussed in Chapter 2, latching relays, in which the current flow closes the relay and latches it in position, can be used to store data. A second current impulse is required to unlatch the relay—hence it is a nonvolatile (permanent) storage. However, relays lack the reliability of other techniques, and are also rather bulky and costly. Nevertheless, thousands of relays were used successfully in early computers— the Harvard University's Mark II had 13,000, and the largest early Bell Telephone computer, 9,000.

Temporary storage is used throughout a computer and is not limited to memory devices. For example a flip-flop, like a relay, remembers (stores) its last state until triggered into changing. A series of flip-flops can be made to store a number, by connecting the stages to make up a register. If lights are made to go on for a 1 but not for a 0, they can also indicate any number.

A *cathode-ray tube* (CRT) stores data in the form of dots on its screen. Because the phosphor brightness decays, the memory is volatile and must be regenerated periodically.

Photographic film, together with the cathode-ray tube, forms a means for rapid storage of large amounts of data. A beam of electrons, modulated by the digital data, is swept across the face of the CRT, and film is moved across the tube face to record the data. Because the film is much wider than the CRT line of light, several lines can be recorded on a single strip. Small dots are recorded at a rate of 10,000 elements per second; and if 50 lines can be recorded on 35-mm film, this is a rate of 500,000 bits per second! Photographic film can be developed and one or more copies printed for later use. A *Selectron* is one type of cathode-ray tube used for information storage.

In computer terminology, electrostatic storage consists of a large matrix of capacitors. Information is stored by the state of each capacitor—for example, a charged capacitor can stand for a 1 and a discharged capacitor for a 0. The electron beam of a CRT can then be used for charging, discharging, or readout.

Other devices, such as punched cards and paper tape, will be discussed in the following chapter on input and output systems.

CHAPTER 11

Input-Output Devices

Ordinary input devices are much too slow for a computer, which works at superhuman speeds. In the fraction of a second it takes to strike a key on a typewriter, for example, a computer can perform hundreds or even thousands of operations. To best use the available computer time, the information must be prepared in advance and stored. Storage forms include paper tape, cards, and magnetic tape.

THE INPUT-OUTPUT PROCESS

Input data for a computer are either fed in manually, are available from instruments or sensors, or are already stored in a form usable by the computer. Using a keyboard, a fast operator can type fifteen to twenty bits a second, which is two or three characters per second in the slowest form of input. Instruments which sense a variable such as pressure or temperature can provide about 10,000 bits per second—about 1000 readings or samples. Finally, computer data can be read from one computer to another at a speed of 60,000 bits, or 10,000 characters, per second. From this it is clear than nonmanual inputs are best from the standpoint of best utilization of computer time.

Input devices can be almost any measuring or reading instrument. Digital data may be used directly, but analog information (as for industrial process computers) must be converted into digital form before it can be used by the computer.

Push buttons and switches are one of the many devices used to place numbers into the computer. Punched tapes and cards are another. A reader senses the holes in the tape or paper and provides corresponding signal outputs. Print readers which scan magnetic ink or printed code letters offer exciting possibilities as computer devices. Present-day equipment can read checks and other documents; and the future promises print readers able to read actual print, just as you are reading this book, and automatically translate the printed words into binary data. Other input devices include magnetic tape readers, and sensors which measure values such as temperature and convert them into binary.

Output devices are in a way the inverse of input devices. The same paper tapes and cards, and magnetic tapes, are used to record the data. There are also other output devices such as typewriters driven by relays which actuate the keys, and visual displays using either lamps or cathode-ray tubes. There are printers that print not only a character, but a line or even a whole page at a time. In some computers, plotters can draw graphs of certain types of outputs, and photographic records can be made of almost any type of output for permanent records.

Every effort is being made to reduce the input-output time in order to make computers even more useful. Fig. 11-1 shows an electronic computer able to read and process a conventional business document. It enables business firms to keep the traditional "hard-copy" records which can be read by employees; yet at the

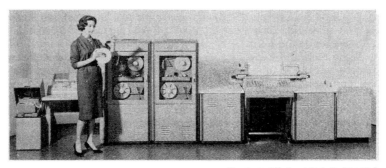

(Courtesy of National Cash Register Co.)

Fig. 11-1. The NCR 390 computer.

same time these records can be used as is for electronic data processing.

The computer in Fig. 11-1 departs from the usual inputs. It uses ordinary ledger cards with four vertical magnetic strips printed on the back. These strips not only "remember" all pertinent data regarding a particular account, but also tell the computer how to handle the account. The front of the ledger card looks like any business form and contains regular printed information.

At the retailing end, cash registers are often linked with punched-tape recorders which automatically preserve on perforated tape a record of each day's transactions. The individual stores then mail the tapes to the home office, where they are processed automatically by the computer.

Using magnetic ledger cards, this computer can prepare a complete payroll, including paychecks and all necessary records, for

109

a firm of 1000 employees in half a working day! Each magnetic ledger card enters into the computer such information as the employee's number, department, exemptions, base pay, overtime, deductions, accumulated earnings and tax credits, etc.

The computer then makes all calculations and prints out the required documents and records, updated and ready for the next day. Essential data are recorded on the back of the ledger cards magnetically, while the front contains the same information in printed form for quick reference and auditing by the personnel.

This computer has a 200-word magnetic-core internal memory, along with internally-stored programs which can be varied at will without the use of pinboards or plugboards. The four types of inputs—magnetic ledger cards, punched cards, punched tape and keyboard—can all be used simultaneously. There are also four output methods, corresponding to the inputs. The punched paper-tape reader can decipher input data at a speed of 400 characters a second. This is equivalent to reading about 3,500 telephone numbers a minute!

Many computers are designed to accept data in only one form, usually magnetic tape. In some computers each input is first converted to magnetic tape before being operated on by the computer. Another popular input, especially for small computers, is the punched paper tape. The computer's task determines the speed at which it must operate and hence the form of input required. A desk computer, for example, would use the slower punched card for reasons of economy.

ANALOG-TO-DIGITAL CONVERSION

Analog data are measured rather than counted. A good example is a voltmeter, which indicates its measured value by the movement of a pointer across a scale.

In business and scientific data processing, almost all information is available in digital form; but there is a large and growing demand for digital computers in process control, where data are not digital. For instance, in a manually-controlled chemical manufacturing process, such as oil refining, the men who operate the system usually read the meters and turn the valves to complete the process. In the automated process of Fig. 11-2, however, readings of temperature, pressure, and rate of flow are obtained by meters at points A, B, and C. Being in analog form, these data must be converted into digital form where a digital computer is to be used. By its program the computer relates these variables and provides control signals to increase the flow at some point, or to turn off the heat at another point. At the same time, a printed record is made for later examination.

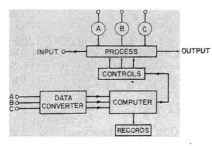

Fig. 11·2. A process control system.

A block diagram of an analog-to-digital converter is shown in Fig. 11-3. Suppose a varying analog input voltage is to be converted into a digital value. This is done by using the sampling technique. The two samples here are A and B, but any others could be taken of course. For sample A, a ramp voltage is applied which starts a clock. The ramp voltage continues to rise until the comparison circuit determines that it has the same value as the sample. An output from the compare block then turns the clock off, and the number of clock pulses represents the ampli-

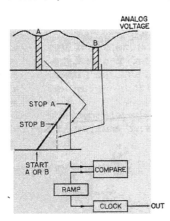

Fig. 11-3. Analog-to-digital conversion.

tude of the sample. For a smaller sample such as B, there will be fewer clock pulses of course. In summary, then, the output from the clock is a series of pulses, the number of which is determined by the input.

Most meters (a voltmeter is one) normally provide an analog scale reading, but new ones have been developed which produce a direct digital readout. In effect, such a meter does its own analog-to-digital conversion and furnishes not only a visual digital reading but a series of digital pulses as well.

111

INPUT DEVICES

Punched-card, paper-tape, and magnetic-tape readers were mentioned briefly at the beginning of the chapter; but it would be a good idea to delve further into these three input devices, to see how they go about feeding a steady diet of information into the computer.

Magnetic Tape Readers

A typical magnetic tape reader (Fig. 11-4) can read 250 characters per inch at a rate of 30,000 characters per second. In many

Fig. 11-4. A magnetic tape handler.

(Courtesy of National Cash Register Co.)

computers, banks of magnetic-tape units are kept and used as a filing system. When a particular piece of information is desired, the computer remembers what to look for, and it skims the magnetic tapes until the data are located. (The technique of tape usage was discussed more fully in Chapter 10.)

Paper Tape

Punched paper tape provides a permanent, nonerasable storage, the data being recorded as holes punched at specific locations. This is another example of a two-valued system, where the indication is either a "hole" or "no hole." Two methods of sensing

112

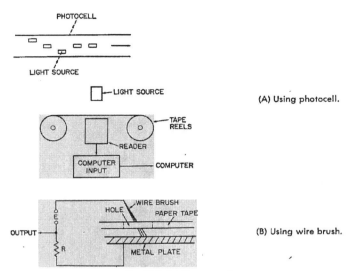

(A) Using photocell.

(B) Using wire brush.

Fig. 11-5. Reading paper tape.

the digits are shown in Fig. 11-5. In Fig. 11-5A a light scans the tape; and wherever there is a hole, the light strikes a photocell underneath which emits an output pulse. A series of cells is required, one for each line of punched holes.

A different technique is shown in Fig. 11-5B. Here a wire brush completes the circuit through the holes to a metal plate underneath.

Punched paper tape from a teletype can easily be converted to computer language by means of a converter and then applied as an input.

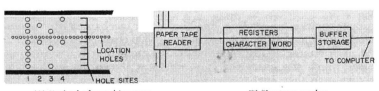

(A) Method of punching tape. (B) The tape reader.

Fig. 11-6. A paper tape reader.

The holes in the paper tape can be located only at pre-determined sites, as shown in Fig. 11-6A. Each set of holes across the tape represents one character. (Four are illustrated in Fig. 11-6A.) A series of characters makes up a word. Location holes guide the tape through the reader (Fig. 11-6B), and also hold it in the

113

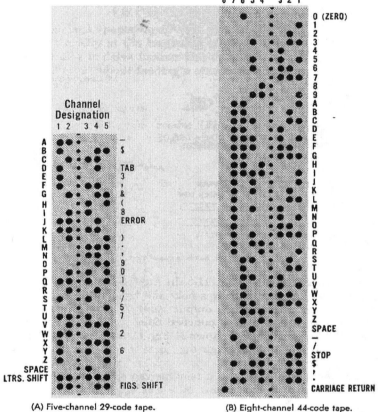

(A) Five-channel 29-code tape.   (B) Eight-channel 44-code tape.

Fig. 11-7. Paper-tape codes.

proper position for reading. Reading, either mechanically or photo-electrically, is done at a speed of about 300 characters per second. At each character the tape is stopped momentarily for reading, after which the character is stored in a temporary register as shown, and then sent to the word register to allow room for the next character. Words are sent to the buffer storage and from there to the computer. Like most buffers, this one saves up the data and sends it to the computer at a faster rate than it is read.

Examples of five- and eight-channel codes are shown in Fig. 11-7. The five-channel tape in Fig. 11-7A uses 29 codes. Like a typewriter, there is a letter and a figure shift to permit printing two characters from one key. The eight-channel tape in Fig. 11-7B uses 44 codes, one for each character.

114

The paper-tape reader in Fig. 11-8 provides the computer with an input of 1,800 characters per second. Parity checks, and two photoelectric readers whose outputs are compared, are used to guard against errors.

Fig. 11-8. A paper-tape reader.

(Courtesy of International Business Machines Corp.)

Punched Cards

Punched cards are used for all kinds of billing, payroll, and other accounting purposes. Almost everyone has seen this type of punched card. IBM cards have 80 columns, and Remington Rand cards have 90. Eighty-column cards have one character per column, with 12 holes on the full width of the card. On a 90-column card there are 12 holes across the card, in two groups of 45 columns each. In putting data on the cards, holes are punched at any of the possible locations, and later read by one of the techniques discussed for paper tape. About 200 cards a minute can be read into a computer. This is 16,000 numbers per minute, far too slow for actual computation. So, punched cards normally are used only for storing input and output information. For use in the computer, this information must first be transferred to another, faster memory.

A number of techniques are used to process the cards. These include *punching*, making holes in the card; *reproducing*, a machine method for sensing the holes on one card and reproducing them on a new card; and *sorting*, or arranging the cards in

115

some sequence. In the third method, key cards are placed in a collator. A deck of cards can then be gone through, and those indicated by the key cards will be selected automatically. The card reader in Fig. 11-9 has a speed of 2,000 cards a minute. Also available is a unit for reading cards and producing tape directly from them.

Fig. 11-9. A punched-card reader.

(Courtesy of National Cash Register Co.)

Print Readers

The ultimate in computer input devices would be one which could read an actual printed page and translate its words into computer language. Believe it or not, such a print reader does exist, in the laboratory stage. This incredible, almost human device scans the printed page with a beam of light. As the light is reflected from each letter or number, the print reader compares the shape with the information in its memory, which in effect contains a series of stencils, one for each letter or number. When a scanned number fits one of the stored stencils in the memory, the proper code symbol is sent to the computer.

The uses for such a machine stagger the imagination. In an office, computers could read, say, an invoice or bill of lading and transfer the information to the memory to provide management with a perpetual, on-the-spot bookkeeping system. Nor is it too fantastic to visualize the newspaper of the future, where reporters would drop their copy into a hopper, to be read, set into type, proofread, and printed automatically. By coupling a print reader to a translator, it would be possible to translate foreign books and newspapers cheaply—a tremendous boon to diplomatic relations. .

116

OUTPUT DEVICES

Output devices translate the results of computation into everyday language understandable by the personnel, or store it on magnetic tape, punched cards, or punched tape for use by the computer. Some of these devices will be discussed in the remainder of the chapter.

Printers

The printer is the basic computer output device. It puts down in black and white the computer results, so they can be read by the personnel.

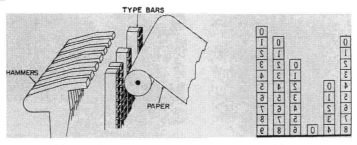

(A) Principle of operation. (B) Type faces.

Fig. 11-10. Gang printing.

The up-and-down movement of the type bars in an ordinary typewriter is far too slow for computers. Moreover, only one letter can be typed at a time. One method of speeding up this operation is shown in Fig. 11-10A. Six type bars, each with the numbers 0 through 9, are raised to the proper position for the desired number (in this example, 840689) and are all struck simultaneously by the hammers. This is the method used by adding machines. Note in Fig. 11-10B that the numbers on the type face are backward so they will print correctly.

A still faster method of printing is illustrated in Fig. 11-11. Here the numbers and characters are placed around the circumference of a wheel. The wheel can be spun much faster than a bar, and need not reverse direction at the end of each stroke. A number of wheels are mounted side by side, enabling a number of characters to be printed simultaneously. All wheels spin in one direction; and when the proper characters are in place, a signal input to the relay then draws the armature, causing the corresponding hammers to strike and print. Even though the wheels spin very rapidly, the hammers strike and lift even faster, and the wheels need not be stopped when struck. This alone greatly increases the speed of printing.

117

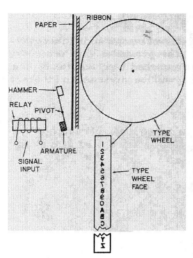

Fig. 11-11. The type-wheel printer.

(Courtesy of Minneapolis-Honeywell Regulator Co.)

Fig. 11-12. The Honeywell 400 high-speed line printer.

A number of wheel printers are available. Some high-speed printers use thyratron drive and can print 24 to 160 characters per line at speeds of up to 2000 lines a minute! The line printer in Fig. 11-12 can print 900 alpha-numeric lines a minute, with up to 120 letters or numbers on each line. This is 108,000 characters —or over 200 single-spaced typewriter pages—a minute!

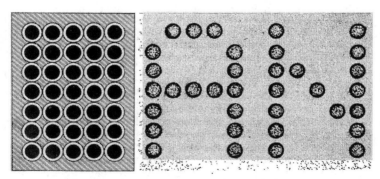

(A) 5 X 7 matrix.   (B) Printed letters.

Fig. 11-13. A wire-matrix printer.

118

Other printers use a matrix of wires. Fig. 11-13A shows a 5 by 7 matrix. As a signal is impressed upon it, the wire burns a small spot on a specially-prepared sensitive paper to form the various letters and numbers. In Fig. 11-13B the letters A and N are given as examples.

Punched Tape

Punched paper tape is used not only to read into computers, as explained previously, but also to provide output information. Unlike magnetic tape, it cannot be erased.

The Friden *Flexowriter* in Fig. 11-14 is a completely automatic writing machine. It reads punched tape, edge-punched cards, or tab cards at the rate of 100 words a minute and, at the same time,

**Fig. 11-14. The Friden SPS "Programatic   Fig. 11-15. Friden auxiliary tape punch.
Flexowriter."**

automatically produces another punched paper tape for future use and types a hard copy for the personnel.

The auxiliary tape punch in Fig. 11-15 permits the *Flexowriter* to punch selected data from two prepunched tapes under control of a third program tape. This output can then be stored and later fed to the *Flexowriter*.

Output Displays

Another form of output is the visual display, often combined with printing. A cathode-ray tube, for example, can display a computer output. One such tube is the *Charactron* shaped-beam tube, which reads out 100,000 computer words per minute! The *Xerox* photocopying process is used to reproduce the information on the screen in permanent form.

As shown in Fig. 11-16, the electron beam from the gun of the *Charactron* is deflected by the selection plates, and passes through the proper character in the matrix. A six-bit code selects the desired character from one of 64 possibilities, and coils keep the

119

beam from scattering. A 20-bit signal then selects the position on the screen where this character is to appear. The display rate is 20,000 characters per second, and the output is "hard copy" printed on paper that can be filed, mailed, or used like any other office record.

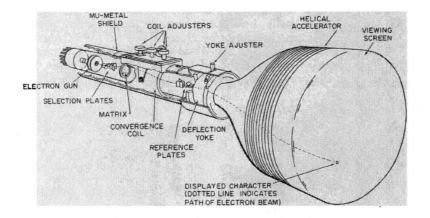

Fig. 11-16. Construction of the "Charactron."

CHAPTER 12

Programming

A computer is a complex arrangement of storage and switching circuits capable of performing certain logical functions such as AND, OR, and NOT. It can add, subtract, multiply, and divide in either the decimal or the binary numbering system; and it can read in or out large quantities of data. But in spite of all this there is one thing a computer cannot do—it is unable to determine what it should do. Incapable of thinking for itself as we humans do, the computer must be told exactly what to do, step by step. This sequence of events is called the *program.*

Programming simply means telling the computer what to do and when to do it—for example, to add A and B, or to divide C by D, or any other step. To evaluate $ax^2 + bx + c$, given a, b, c, and x, the computer might follow this simplified program:

1. Read a, b, c, and x into the memory.
2. Read x from the memory into the portion of the main register which is for temporary storage.
3. Multiply x by x to get x^2, and then multiply by a to get ax^2.
4. Store ax^2.
5. Read b into the main register and multiply by x to get bx.
6. Add ax^2, from the memory, to bx in the register; the register now contains $ax^2 + bx$.
7. Add c so the register has $ax^2 + bx + c$.
8. Store $ax^2 + bx + c$ in the memory for later use.

These steps constitute a short program for computer action. Another example might be to program a magnetic-drum readout. Five steps are necessary:

1. Temporarily store the address of the word to be read out.
2. Convert the address into a signal which will give the track on which the word is located and its position on the track.
3. Using this signal, first select the proper track.
4. By means of the timing pulses, count the words until the beginning of the desired word is reached.
5. Read this word into the proper register for later operations. Stop reading at the end of the word.

121

STORED PROGRAMS

The first digital computer was the abacus, used by the ancient Greeks and Romans and even today by many shopkeepers in China. This relatively simple device consists of parallel wires on which are strung beads, each wire representing a column of figures. Despite its simplicity, it is claimed that an expert abacus operator can compute faster than a person using a calculator. Since the beads are moved from one end of the wire to the other, the abacus can be said to have a form of storage. This elementary type of storage was the prototype of the digital computer, in which relays and pulses take the place of the beads.

The first automatic computer was designed by Charles Babbage in 1833. Called an analytical engine, it was controlled by punched cards so that its operations occurred in sequence. Since the program was in the cards, external to the computer, it was an externally-programmed machine. Remarkable for its time, Babbage's computer was never built because the production problems were too great and his support was too small.

Harvard's Mark 1, the Automatic Sequence Controlled Calculator completed in 1944, uses relays for internal operation and punched paper tape for external programming. The first all-electronic computer, ENIAC (for Electronic Numerical Integrator and Computer), was completed at the University of Pennsylvania in 1946. ENIAC uses wiring plugboards and switches for its program. All of these computers store their programs outside the computer, and use their internal memory only for the numbers in the actual computation.

Modern computers are stored-program machines in which the internal memory retains all the steps needed for problem solution. The magnetic-core memory, first used in the UNIVAC II and in the IBM 704 and 705, is still the most common type of memory in modern computers because of its flexibility and speed.

Each step in the program is an instruction, and within each instruction are codes for the individual actions (for example, 17 may mean add, and 13, subtract). Thus, a program is all the steps and planning required to guide the computer through a problem, the instructions or commands are individual steps which are followed in sequence, and coding is the translation of instructions into computer language.

In a simple task, the program may tell the control circuit to look to address 1439, where a number (or computer word) is stored. This number is read to the control circuit, which has been instructed to add this number to the one already at another address, 2163. This address is the accumulator (AC), the section of the memory reserved for arithmetic operations.

122

INSTRUCTIONS

In a stored-program computer, a magnetic-core memory stores the program steps or instructions in sequence, as described in Chapter 10. With a memory plane 64 by 64, there will be 4096 individual locations. By numbering each core from 0 to 4096, each location will thus have an address. Each word is 10 digits long, so there are 10 planes. Hence, each address actually means one core location, but 10 cores deep.

An address such as 1304 is only a location. At each location there is a computer word, either an instruction or a number for computation. (Instructions and numbers both appear as binary numbers, but decimal numbers will be used in the following discussion, for convenience.) A number such as 3571 may be stored at the 2153rd location or address, awaiting instructions.

	LOCATION	CODE	(MEANS)	ADDRESS
A	675	11	ADD	1306
B	342	01	STORE-AC	1500
C	343	10	ADD-AC	1571
D	344	11	STORE	1634

Fig. 12-1. Typical program codes.

A series of instructions is shown in Fig. 12-1. Instruction A, as an example, tells us that the computer is following a series of instructions—the last one was 674, the present one is 675, and the next one is 676. Two parts make up this instruction, the code and the address. Code 11 here means "add," and 1306 is the address of the number to be added. Hence, 111306 means "add the number whose location is 1306." A control circuit takes the first two digits, 11, reads "add," then looks into address 1306 to see what to add. This is a single-address instruction; there are other, more complex ones.

Three additional instructions are shown in B, C, and D of Fig. 12-1. The instructions at B tell the computer memory to send the next instruction, located at address 342. This instruction arrives as 011500. The control circuits then decode this number. The first bits (01) are the "store AC" code, which means "take the number located at 1500 and store it in the accumulator (AC) register."

The next instruction (343) is 101571, or "add the number at 1571 to the contents of the accumulator." Now the accumulator has the sum of the numbers formerly located at 1500 and 1571. Step D means store this sum in location 1634.

Multiplying is a multiple-step process. Suppose, as in Fig. 12-2, the multiplicand is 12 and the multiplier is 21. Hence, there will be a four-digit answer, or product. As discussed in Chapter 5, multiplication is a series of add and shift operations, and three instructions will be required as shown. The first instruction is 037, which has a code 24 meaning "load M." This tells the computer to take the number (12) at location 1521, and put it into register M as shown.

Step 2, or 038, has code 43 meaning "multiply." Address 1673 is also given at this time, meaning "multiply the number now in the accumulator by the number at address 1673." The latter number is 21, the multiplier, which is placed in the multiplier register.

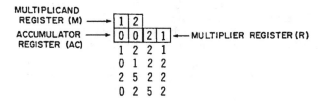

LOCATION	CODE	(MEANS)	ADDRESS
037	24	LOAD M	1521
038	43	MULTIPLY	1673
039	11	STORE	3471

Fig. 12-2. Multiplication instruction codes.

The accumulator register has room in this example for only two digits; and since the products will have four, the accumulator and multiplier are placed together to make a four-place register.

The accumulator register (AC) and multiplier register (R) now have 0021, while M has 12. The last digit of R is a 1 which the control circuits read and, following instructions, add 12 to 0021 once to get 1221. This partial product is then shifted right, resulting in 0122. Because of the last 2, the contents of M (the number 12) are added to 0122 twice to yield 2522. When shifted right this is 252.

Now the product is in AC and R, and the multiplier is gone. Instruction 039 (code 14) is to take the product and store it in location 3471. Note that these shifts are purely a mechanical process for this technique of multiplication. It is still necessary to shift the complete number left to multiply by 2, and right to divide by 2.

In this chapter six different codes have been established. Their computer meanings are as follows: 01 (Store AC), take the number from the address given and store it in AC; 10 (Add AC), take the number from the designated address and add it to the

124

contents of AC; 11 (Store), take the number from accumulator AC and store it at the designated address; 24 (Load M), take the number located at the address given and place in multiplier register M; 43 (Multiply), take the number given at the proper address and multiply by the contents of M. There are, of course, many other possible codes.

Fig. 12-3 shows a series of actual commands (instructions) used in the *Libratrol 500* process control computer. The computer, operating on the input information supplied by the program, performs the computations, logic manipulation, and decision making required to produce the control actions. Its operation is serial, single-address, fixed-binary point with an internally-stored program.

CODE LETTER OF COMMAND	COMMAND	EXPLANATION
B	Bring	Replace the contents of the accumulator with the contents of memory location m.
A	Add	Add contents of m to the contents of the accumulator, and retain the sum in the accumulator.
S	Subtract	Subtract the contents of m from the contents of the accumulator, and retain the difference in the accumulator.
M	Multiply, Fractional	Multiply the number in the accumulator by the number in memory location m, terminating the result at 30 binary places and retaining the most significant half of the product in the accumulator.
N	Multiply Integral	Multiply the number in the accumulator by the number in memory location m, retaining the least significant half of the product in the accumulator.
D	Divide	Divide the number in the accumulator by the number in memory location m, retaining the quotient (rounded to 30 bits) in the accumulator.
H	Hold	Store contents of the accumulator in m, retaining the number in the accumulator.
C	Clear	Store contents of the accumulator in memory location m, clearing the accumulator.
Y	Store Address	Store only the address part of the word in the accumulator in memory location m, leaving the rest of the word in m undisturbed. (Useful when the operator wishes to modify the address portion of an instruction.)

Fig. 12-3. Command codes for the "Libratrol 500" process control computer.

Inputs to the computer are derived from standard-process instrumentation, in the form of voltages from analog instruments, digitized transducer signals, and similar information provided by the operating personnel.

A block diagram of this computer is shown in Fig. 12-4. Since it is designed for process control, there are voltage inputs from sensors (discussed in Chapter 11), operator inputs, and pulse data to be counted. Outputs include a *Flexowriter* for producing typed copy or punched paper tape, several digital outputs for contacts in the controlled process, and several control voltages available through digital-to-analog conversion to points in the process under control.

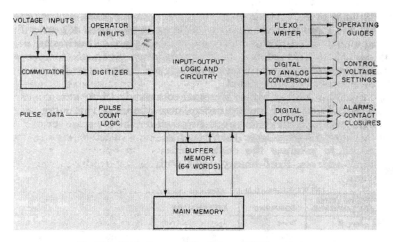

VOLTAGE INPUTS

OPERATOR INPUTS

COMMUTATOR → DIGITIZER

PULSE DATA → PULSE COUNT LOGIC

INPUT-OUTPUT LOGIC AND CIRCUITRY

FLEXO-WRITER → OPERATING GUIDES

DIGITAL TO ANALOG CONVERSION → CONTROL VOLTAGE SETTINGS

DIGITAL OUTPUTS → ALARMS, CONTACT CLOSURES

BUFFER MEMORY (64 WORDS)

MAIN MEMORY

Fig. 12-4. Block diagram of the "Libratrol 500" computer.

Instructions are in the form of words which include data for computation and instructions for operation. The only difference is in how the computer uses this information; each system has its

PARITY	S	DATA PORTION																								
27	26	25	24	23	22	21	20	19	18	17	16	15	14	13	12	11	10	9	8	7	6	5	4	3	2	1

MSB   LSB

(A) Basic internal data word.

S	DIGIT 6	DIGIT 5	DIGIT 4	DIGIT 3	DIGIT 2	DIGIT 1
25	24 23 22 21	20 19 18 17	16 15 14 13	12 11 10 9	8 7 6 5	4 3 2 1

(B) Digital-data word format.

S	DIGIT 4	DIGIT 3	DIGIT 2	DIGIT 1
25	24 23 22 21 20 19 18 17	16 15 14 13 12 11 10 9	8 7 6 5	4 3 2 1

(C) Alpha-numeric data word format.

S	24-BIT BINARY NUMBER
25	24 23 22 21 20 19 18 17 16 15 14 13 12 11 10 9 8 7 6 5 4 3 2 1

S = SIGN

(D) Binary data word format.

Fig. 12-5. Make-up of the UNIVAC III 27-bit word.

own method for producing words. IBM's 1620 two-address instruction format reduces the number of instructions required to perform an operation, thus simplifying the programming of the system and reducing the amount of storage required. For example, *one* instruction will locate, add, and store the sum of two numbers, or transmit from one location to another an entire record regardless of length. For a two-address instruction, the locations of both addresses are given in the instruction.

UNIVAC III, for example, uses a 27-bit word, 2 parity bits, and 25 information bits, as in Fig. 12-5A. The least significant bits (LSB) are on the right, and the most significant bits (MSB), on the left. For digital-data word format, six 4-bit numbers plus the sign make up a word as in Fig. 12-5B; four 6-bit alpha-numeric digits make up a combination of letters and numbers as in Fig. 12-5C; and Fig. 12-5D shows the binary-data word format which can represent any positive or negative binary value from 0 to 16,777,215. Instructions in UNIVAC III use six bits for the operation code and ten for the single address, along with other uses for the rest of the bits.

	TYPE	EXAMPLE											
A	NUMERIC	±	1	2	3	4	5	6	7	8	9	0	1
B	ALPHA-NUMERIC	R	O		B	I		N	S		O		N
C	ALPHA-NUMERIC COMPRESSED	C	•		W	E		B	B		1	7	4
D	BINARY	±	(44 BINARY DIGITS)										
E	INSTRUCTION	OPERATION CODE		ADDRESS A		ADDRESS B		ADDRESS C					
F	FLOATING POINT	± EXPONENT (7 BINARY DIGITS)		MANTISSA (40 BINARY DIGITS)									

Fig. 12-6. Word structure for the Honeywell 800 computer.

In the Honeywell *800* computer a word (Fig. 12-6) has 54 bits —6 for checking to prevent errors, and 48 information bits. These may be used as in A to represent an 11-decimal digit number plus sign; or several smaller decimal numbers, each with its own sign. Using coding, these 48 bits can also represent eight alphabetic characters as in B, or a combination of letters and numbers as in C. Binary, as shown in D, is carried as 44 binary digits plus the sign. E shows the word divided into four 12-bit portions—the operation code plus three addresses. This makes up an instruction whose three-address form might be; "add the number at address A to the number at address B and store the result at address C."

The exponential notation of numbers makes it possible to write them as values between 1 and 10 together in the exponential notation, as shown in F. Thus, the 48 bits represent a sign, the exponent of 10, and the number or mantissa.

AUTOMATIC PROGRAMS

A number of simplified types of computer language such as RCA's COBOL (Common Business-Oriented Language) have been developed for greater ease in programming. These are not actually automatic programs, but special symbols and commands. Short, specialized programs, or subroutines, which are used many times are stored in a library of programs and called into use as required.

Some programming systems which have such subroutines are COBOL, SPS (IBM's Symbolic Programming System), FORTRAN (Formula translation), and others.

FORTRAN, designed for engineering and research calculations, uses written algebraic and English notations. Programs are written in the form of equations which are compiled automatically into an efficient computer program designed for and compatible with IBM data-processing systems.